HONDURAS

WESTVIEW PROFILES
NATIONS OF CONTEMPORARY LATIN AMERICA
Ronald M. Schneider, Series Editor

Honduras: Caudillo Politics and Military Rulers,
James A. Morris

†*Mexico: Paradoxes of Stability and Change,*
Daniel Levy and Gabriel Székely

†*Nicaragua: The Land of Sandino,* Thomas W. Walker

†*The Dominican Republic: A Caribbean Crucible,*
Howard J. Wiarda and Michael J. Kryzanek

Colombia: Portrait of Unity and Diversity, Harvey F. Kline

Also of Interest

†*Latin America, Its Problems and Its Promise:*
An Interdisciplinary Introduction,
edited by Jan Knippers Black

†*The Caribbean Challenge: U.S. Policy in a Volatile Region,*
edited by H. Michael Erisman

†*The End and the Beginning: The Nicaraguan Revolution,* John A. Booth

†*Revolution in El Salvador: Origins and Evolution,*
Tommie Sue Montgomery

†*Revolution in Central America,*
edited by the Stanford Central America Action Network

Political Change in Central America: Internal and External Dimensions,
edited by Wolf Grabendorff, Heinrich-W. Krumwiede, and Jörg Todt

†*The New Cuban Presence in the Caribbean,* edited by Barry B. Levine

†Available in hardcover and paperback.

HONDURAS

Caudillo Politics and Military Rulers

James A. Morris

Westview Press / Boulder and London

Westview Profiles / Nations of Contemporary Latin America

All photos are copyrighted by Seven Goats Photography—James Morris.

Published in 1984 in the United States of America by Westview Press, Inc., 5500 Central Avenue, Boulder, Colorado 80301; Frederick A. Praeger, President and Publisher

Library of Congress Cataloging in Publication Data
Morris, James A., 1938–
    Honduras: caudillo politics and military rulers.
    (Nations of contemporary Latin America)
    Bibliography: p.
    Includes index.
    1. Honduras—Politics and government—1933– .
2. Civil-military relations—Honduras. 3. Honduras—
Armed Forces—Political activity. 4. Honduras—
Economic policy. I. Title. II. Series.
F1508.M67 1984   322′.5′097283   83-21789
ISBN 0-86531-178-1

Printed and bound in the United States of America

10   9   8   7   6   5   4   3   2   1

DEDICATED TO MY PARENTS

Alvin Francis Morris

Lorraine Elizabeth Morris

Contents

Tables and Illustrations

ix

PHOTO SECTION FOLLOWING P. 73:

A woman wearing a souvenir of a Liberal Party
political campaign

A sample of major Honduran newspapers

The presidential house

Statue of Honduran writer, politician, and philosopher
José Cecilio del Valle in Tegucigalpa

Parque Leona overlooking downtown Tegucigalpa

The church at Valle de Angeles

The Municipal Market of Santa Rosa de Copán

A small-town general store

Mt. Picacho is a backdrop for central Tegucigalpa

Foreword

Recent experience has taught us that just because a country such as Honduras is small and has never played a major role in hemispheric—much less global—affairs, we cannot assume that it is unimportant. Brazil, Mexico, Argentina, and Colombia notwithstanding, most of the countries of Latin America are small and with little weight in international affairs. Indeed, this is the case with a decided majority of the world's countries. Then, too, Honduras has been overshadowed because it is located between Central American countries that enjoy greater prominence for one reason or another: Guatemala on the north, larger and scene of a turbulent revolutionary experience between 1944 and 1954; Nicaragua to the south, locale of a controversial ongoing revolution; and El Salvador on the west, racked by protracted civil war. To the east lies the Caribbean—itself scarcely a sea of tranquillity. Given Honduras's location and the ever-increasing U.S. presence there, the world will certainly hear much more of this nation and its people in the years immediately ahead.

James Morris knows and understands Honduras as do very few persons who have not spent their lifetimes there. His book not only puts the country in comparative perspective but also demonstrates how contemporary military regimes have roots in the *caudillismo* of earlier eras. As with the other studies in this series, this volume is an interpretive essay even more than a compendium of relevant information. It portrays a society undergoing change on many fronts, albeit limited in rate and extent; an essentially agrarian economy that supports a growing urban service sector on a precariously limited industrial base; and a political system riddled with contradictions between partially undermined traditional institutions and processes and as yet extremely fragile and oftentimes rootless features of a modern party and interest-group infrastructure.

The author's approach is basically that of cultural relativism tempered with a residual pluralist democratic orientation, and his most important analytical concept is that of the "cycle of political frustration" as a pattern repeated several times during a slowly ascending developmental experience. This is now aggravated by the political polarization of Central America between Marxists and authoritarian conservative forces, so the next cycle—perhaps already under way—will be complicated by the end of Honduras's relative international remoteness, with Central America a cold-war cockpit rather than a backwater region. Morris's study leaves the reader well prepared to comprehend the critical events of the mid-1980s in the center of Central America.

If in this book culture receives little attention relative to other books in this series, it is because there is far less that is distinctive or of note in this sphere of Honduran national life. By way of contrast, international affairs, particularly relations with other Central American countries, are treated in detail, a fact of great importance since the Reagan administration has clearly chosen to make Honduras into the major U.S. military base in the area. Indeed, it is this small country's fast-growing role as a base for operations against the Sandinista regime in Nicaragua and for training of El Salvador's military that makes Professor Morris's well-informed study a particularly timely and significant addition to the Nations of Contemporary Latin America series.

Ronald M. Schneider

Preface

In the classic 1950 study by William S. Stokes, the Republic of Honduras is described as having a highly centralized political structure based on authoritarian propensities and personalistic modes of individual and societal relationships. Despite a variety of changes that have transformed the society, centralization, authoritarianism, and personalism remain as primary characteristics of Honduran society and politics. *Caudillismo,* or political bossism and strong-man rule, has, in some aspects, been followed by the predominance of military rule. Even so, traditional social and political values have perpetuated the concept that control over the state and appropriation of its resources are legitimate means of social mobility or personal gain. It is questionable whether the "ventures of successful pillage" led by the caudillos (the political bosses) of old and the corruption that has accompanied military rule are functionally different or whether new social and institutional conditions have merely determined a new technique.

Continuity of the political order has been preserved, but both old and new elites must now contend with aspects of social, cultural, economic, and political change—all part of rapid modernization and socioeconomic development. Through decades of national fragmentation, dictatorship, institutional weakness, and the consolidation of military rule, elements of traditional caudillo politics have persisted and survived. It is doubtful, however, whether continued military political dominance will provide the institutional formula Hondurans need to forge the consensus required to address the nation's social and economic problems. Both these tasks—political consensus and national development—have been influenced greatly by global and regional phenomena, especially the unfolding crisis in Central America.

Given the contemporary attention focused upon Central America, it is perhaps difficult to understand the previous isolation of Honduras from both world events and the literature of North and South America. My principal question about Honduras in 1970 was whether the country had *any* organized "interest groups," and, if so, what they were and how they functioned. In the decade or so since, a few scholars have quietly pursued their studies of the country with little or no institutional support. Significantly, this volume represents the first comprehensive study of Honduras to be published (in English) since that of Stokes. In the wake of crisis and revolution in Central America, more essays, articles, and books on the region and the countries within it are destined to appear. However, our understanding of just what is occurring in those countries is uneven, weak, or nonexistent in many respects. This study attempts to partially fill that void, but much remains to be explored and examined.

One of the most significant developments to occur over the last decade or so has been the emergence and growth of studies produced by Hondurans. Trained in Europe, the United States, Costa Rica, and elsewhere in Latin America, Honduran scholars are actively applying new methodologies toward the study of their own society, its history, and various facets of social and economic change. These scholars and their published works represent a critical mass in the evolution of knowledge about Honduras. Future research on the country will increasingly involve the collaboration of both Honduran and North American students. I would expect both communities to benefit greatly.

This book indeed represents the labors and thoughts of scholars and others in Honduras and North America. Invaluable guidance and introductions to the Honduran "family" were provided by Teresa Castilla Blanca, Rosita de Velásquez de Vare, and Mario Posas. To them, and many other Hondurans who gave of their time, energy, hospitality, and insight, I express my gratitude and hopes for the future.

My appreciation is extended to the many colleagues who either read portions of the manuscript or offered their ideas and suggestions gained from their own trips to Central America. In particular, I wish to thank Edward Boatman-Guillán, Cal Clark, Rosemary Davis, former Ambassador Mari-Luci Jaramillo, Stuart Lippe, Martin Needler, Neale Pearson, Karen Remmer, Mark Rosenberg, and James Torres, as well as Steve C. Ropp and José Z. Garcia of the Central American Working Group at New Mexico State University.

In the end, however, this book was made possible by the "bread and shelter" and emotional support extended by the Ropp family of Las Cruces, the Garcia family of El Paso, the Morris family of Santa Cruz, and all those who remembered in Albuquerque.

James A. Morris

1

Caudillos, Enclaves, and Political Uncertainty, 1876–1956

While exploring the New World during his fourth voyage (1502–1504), Christopher Columbus touched upon the Caribbean island of Guanaja off the northern coast of Honduras. Landing on the Central American mainland at a point now called Cabo de Honduras near the present city of Trujillo, he claimed the territory for the Spanish Crown. Later, when the explorers rounded the Cape of Gracias a Dios near the Honduran-Nicaraguan frontier, a storm threatened the fleet's safety, and Columbus is reputed to have expressed his thanks to God after they had escaped the storm-tossed watery depths (or *honduras*), thus giving the cape its name. The region left behind, then known as Higueras, was sparsely populated with nomadic Indian tribes, and it was nearly twenty years later before Spain renewed its interest.

As part of the Captain-Generalcy of Guatemala, Honduras was located on the fringes of the Spanish colonial empire. It was not until 1786 that Spain created the Intendancy of Comayagua. This marked the beginning of a regional rivalry between Comayagua and Tegucigalpa. The former was the seat of colonial authority and then the republican capital until 1880 when Tegucigalpa, riding the crest of a revived silver-mining boom, became the political capital of Honduras. The latter city was first settled near the end of the sixteenth century, when silver deposits were discovered nearby.[1] Though the silver mines were the most important in Central America, scarcity of labor and the exhaustion of the veins had left them practically dormant at the end of the 1700s. The colonial experience of Honduras was one of neglect due to such things as lack of interest by the Spanish Crown, administrative ineffi-ciency, and more urgent concerns elsewhere within the colonial realm. Geographical isolation and the physical ruggedness of Honduras also limited penetration into the region. Scarcity of labor, lack of appropriate

1

technology, and nonexistent infrastructure hampered the development of mining and other types of industry. To further weaken Spanish influence, the Catholic church never acquired extensive wealth or power in Honduras.[2]

The colonial provinces of Central America declared their independence in 1821. The region never became involved in a war of liberation, but merely took advantage of Mexico's revolt against Spain. The United Provinces of Central America were unable to consolidate a confederated system of government, and after several years of intraregional rivalry the union collapsed. In January 1839, Honduras became the second province (after Nicaragua) to declare itself a separate state. There followed a series of frustrating attempts at reunification, mostly with Nicaragua and El Salvador. Guatemala, however, dominated regional affairs, and events in Honduras were influenced by Guatemalan intervention and support for rival factions. The transfer of power in Honduras more often than not was disorderly and violent, except in 1852 when José Trinidad Cabañas peacefully assumed the presidency. The first half century of independence was a period filled with turbulence, regional disunity, and the absence of national perceptions. An ephemeral nationalism and the lack of a strong and cohesive ruling class (oligarchy) left Honduras open to outside interference and exploitation by international intrigue and economic interests.

ERA OF LIBERAL REFORMS

During the 1870s, the Liberal-Conservative battles of Central America were resolved in favor of the Liberals. In Honduras, the era was launched with the presidency of Marco Aurelio Soto (1876–1883). New ideas about economic development were introduced, the state became more supportive of entrepreneurial ventures, and public lands were made available for private purchase or homesteading. New economic policies were decreed to stimulate both domestic and foreign investment in Honduras, as Liberal leaders sought to modernize the country's economic structures. Technology and capital were needed, and most would have to be imported one way or another.[3]

By 1880, a new constitution had been put together, and codes had been decreed regulating commerce, customs, mining, penal affairs, and the military. The separation of church and state was reinforced by the expropriation of church property and banishment of tithes. Control of the cemeteries was transferred to local governments (*municipios*). Monetary stabilization policies were drawn up, and President Soto established the Casa de Moneda. Tax exemptions were granted, and national lands were often granted as part of investment agreements. Foreign investors, especially mining and banana-plantation developers, were to obtain generous concessions. The long-range strategy of Honduran leaders was to promote agricultural development. With the export of agricultural

Statue of Honduran military hero Francisco Morazán, who governed the Central American Union from 1829 until 1838.

surpluses the country would then be able to finance imports of goods, machinery, and technology.

Throughout the nineteenth century, the Honduran economy—although varied and relatively self-sufficient—was disaggregated. Production was at subsistence levels, and contact with world markets was minimal. These conditions added to the isolation of Honduras and allowed the country's archaic social and economic structures to linger on well into the twentieth century. In contrast, coffee-growing elites in Guatemala, El Salvador, and Costa Rica had been able to consolidate their positions economically and politically. Those national economies relied upon coffee exports to finance imports and some programs of national development. In the wake of Liberal reforms, Honduras attempted to emulate its neighbors, but coffee production did not truly develop until well after World War II. Thus, a solid ruling class did not emerge that was able to support or even benefit from the expansion of exports. The policy of favorable land concessions, new commercial codes, and the willingness of the state to accept foreign capital on liberalized terms all led to higher levels of foreign investment in mining and agricultural enterprises, so that international economic interests eventually dominated production within the Honduran export sector. Since coffee production was minimal and grew slowly, the mining and fruit companies were alone in their ability to provide the country an export capacity. It was through foreign-controlled enterprises, for the most part, that Honduras was first integrated into the expanding capitalist world market.

With Liberal reform, the Honduran mining sector was revived with British, French, North American, and some Honduran capital. The new codes established a series of concessions and privileges for investors, including lands, rights of way, free import of goods and machinery, and other tax exemptions. In 1880, the New York and Honduras Rosario Mining Company was organized and obtained its first twenty-year concession from the government.[4] Regardless of these efforts, by the end of the nineteenth century the mining industry had once again declined as financial problems, falling silver prices, and unpromising claim sites contributed to a rash of business failures.

INTRODUCTION OF THE BANANA INDUSTRY

The decline in mining activity coincided and merged with the ascendance of the banana industry. North American investors began to build plantations along the northern coast of Honduras under terms similar to those granted to mining concessions. Commerce in bananas and other tropical produce had originated in the Bay Islands during the 1860s and 1870s. Ships made occasional visits to Roatán to take on extra cargo that was profitable in New Orleans and eastern seaboard cities of the United States. Until just after the turn of the century, banana production in Honduras depended on numerous small, independent producers, and competition among them was advantageous for produce buyers. Though cultivation was predominately by Hondurans, access to markets and overseas transport were in the hands of foreign shippers and brokers.

Improvement in shipping and regular schedules helped to increase banana exports. By 1892, bananas constituted nearly 12 percent of all Honduran exports. The next thirty years brought dramatic growth to this industry along the North Coast, transforming the region into a dynamic economic zone that provided new revenues for the state. From 1890 to 1930, the production of bananas, mostly by U.S. companies, catapulted Honduras into the position of the world's leading banana exporter. It was during this "golden age" that major foreign investments were made in the departments of Cortés, Atlántida, and Colón.[5]

By the second decade of the twentieth century, three companies dominated production and marketing in Honduras. In 1899, the Vaccaro family—which had been plying the fruit trade between Central America and New Orleans—was successful in receiving a concession to develop lands in the Aguán River valley along the northeastern coast of Honduras. In 1904, the Vaccaros and their partner obtained another concession, valid for seventy-five years, in which they acquired lands in exchange for the construction of railroads. This contract exempted the Vaccaro Fruit Company from many contemporary and future taxes. In 1926, an array of enterprises under the aegis of the Vaccaros was consolidated into the Standard Fruit and Steamship Company.

Along the western portion of the Honduran coast near Omoa, another land concession of 2,024 hectares on both sides of the Cuyamel River was granted to William F. Streich in 1902. Streich later sold his failing business to a more aggressive entrepreneur whose subsequent exploits lend a colorful page or two to Honduran history. At first, Samuel Zemurray's business dealings were supported by the prosperous multinational United Fruit Company; but by 1911, Zemurray was able to organize the Cuyamel Fruit Company, free of financial entanglements with United. Part of Zemurray's success was due to the realization by government officials that he represented the only serious competition to the United Fruit Company. It was deemed desirable to avoid monopoly control over what was now an important source of state revenue. In addition, the leader of Cuyamel was fully involved in presidential politics, especially the revolt that placed Manuel Bonilla into the presidency (1912–1913). In 1912, Cuyamel received a long-term lease on another 10,000 hectares of land.

The largest and most powerful banana company was, and still is, the United Fruit Company (now United Brands). A Boston-based businessman, Minor C. Keith, merged his various produce-import operations to form United Fruit. Honduran subsidiaries were the Truxillo Railroad and the Tela Railroad companies, named for the North Coast ports from which their produce was shipped. United Fruit became an even more preponderant economic and political force when it absorbed Zemurray's Cuyamel in 1929. For his part, the resourceful Zemurray ended up as United's director of tropical operations.

By the end of the 1920s, the banana companies had control over large expanses of the most fertile lands in northern Honduras and employed around twenty-two thousand workers. The foreign-owned companies operated—and in effect owned—the railroads, including the National Railroad that ran 100 kilometers from Puerto Cortés to Potrerillos.[6] The docks and ships were also part of the network of foreign investments. The companies owned local electric facilities, ice plants, communications systems, sugar mills, commissaries, and soap factories, as well as the largest, most important bank in the country.

The expansion of the banana industry opened up the isolated and difficult-to-settle littoral along the northern coast. Foreign investors brought needed infrastructure development, introduced agricultural technology, and helped provide public works and other services to growing towns and cities such as San Pedro Sula, Puerto Cortés, Tela, El Progreso, and La Ceiba. Thousands of jobs were created, along with a general economic stimulus that spread throughout the North Coast region. Although the state had supplied the conditions for new and expanded investments, the country was unable to finance the opportunities that were created. In the context of an expanding capitalist world economy, foreigners were more able to take advantage of the investment opportunities than were Hondurans. The long-term impact on Honduran social and economic development posed contradictory issues for the country's economic and political evolution.

One consequence was a reduction in the number of independent Honduran banana growers. Transport and overseas marketing were controlled by the foreign-owned companies, so that growers were often forced to sell their properties at bargain rates or at least accommodate their operations to those of the fruit companies. The companies also built the rail lines primarily to meet their needs of transporting produce to the ports of Trujillo, La Ceiba, Tela, and Puerto Cortés, with the long-range consequence being the failure to develop major routes of transport connecting the dynamic North Coast region with the mountainous interior of Honduras.

As the North Coast economy grew, its labor needs expanded. Workers were brought from Jamaica, the Cayman Islands, and the Lesser Antilles to work on the railroads, operate the docks, and harvest fruit. This external source of immigration was complemented by the arrival of Honduran migrants from the more densely populated western part of the country. New towns sprang up, and the larger towns such as La Ceiba and San Pedro Sula became busy commercial centers. Urbanization and the environment of the work place produced conditions that were to lead eventually to the formation of an organized working class.[7]

More generalized consequences of mining and the banana plantations concern the failure of Honduras to develop a strong ruling class that might have been more able to defend the country's economic and political interests. As mentioned earlier, national economic and governing classes—the so-called coffee elites—had been consolidated by the mid-nineteenth century in El Salvador and Guatemala, and to a lesser extent in Nicaragua and Costa Rica. The rapid expansion of foreign investment into Honduras around the turn of the century displaced local entrepreneurs and inhibited the formation of a national economic elite. Honduran political and economic elites were enlisted by the foreign-owned enterprises as employees or consultants. Working for the multinational corporations or acting as an intermediary between business and government became the principal means of social and economic mobility. Thus to a great extent the perspectives of the Honduran ruling classes were shaped by their relationship as "clients" of the banana companies. Their economic fortunes and not infrequently their political welfare became linked to the activities of the export economy, and as such their political and economic autonomy was limited.

The alliance between foreign capital and the landholding elites paralleled the "duality" of the Honduran economy. The traditional precapitalist economic and social structures of rural Honduras coexisted with the export sector that was limited geographically to the North Coast. The coastal region had evolved as an "enclave" society. As an economy it had added to infrastructure development, provided new sources of revenue for the state, and to some degree increased capitalization of the national economy, but on the whole had not had an integrative or stimulating effect upon Honduran development outside the North Coast.[8] Most of the development that did occur was localized and benefited the export sectors.

Though perhaps defined by capitalistic/precapitalistic distinctions, the boundaries of the enclave economy and society were not the only barriers to Honduran national integration. Social and political fragmentation also was reflected in the relative absence of an established aristocracy, or sense of class interest, that had developed in other parts of Central America. Rather, the status, economic well-being, and social mobility of Honduran governing elites became intertwined with the growth of the state and its dependence upon an externally controlled export sector. The ruling groups that did emerge competed for the wealth and political resources offered by the large foreign-owned corporations. The alliance between political caudillos and foreign interests inhibited the evolution of any coherent vision among political leaders that emphasized national interests.

THE CARÍAS YEARS

The personalistic mode of politics and the disposition to engage in compromising relationships presented United Fruit and other foreign investors several opportunities to gain access to the state and to cement relations within the class of governing elites. Throughout the 1920s, politicians of the Liberal Party of Honduras (PLH) became concerned about the economic power increasingly exercised by the United Fruit Company. Liberal leaders therefore promoted the Cuyamel Fruit Company to offset growing monopoly control, and Cuyamel evolved as one of the Liberal party's principal financial supporters. This situation changed drastically when Zemurray sold Cuyamel to the "octopus"—that is, United Fruit.

United meanwhile had embarked on a long-term strategy of cultivating its own coterie of Honduran political elites.[9] The company decided to back Tiburcio Carías Andino, an aspiring caudillo politician who had become a central figure in the National Party of Honduras (PNH). By weaving personal loyalties into extended relationships and using the backing of United Fruit Company resources, Carías was able to fashion a power base through which he was eventually able to extend his influence over most of Honduras. In 1932, United's efforts were rewarded when the National party faction headed by Carías won office.

"Barring the possibility of a rebellion, the new executive will take office on February 1, 1929, for a term of four years." This news account, although speculative, reflected the political disunity and rivalry that had plagued Honduras since the dissolution of the original Central American confederation in 1838. Early electoral campaigns were considered and directed as battles, and caudillos regarded the opposition as the enemy. The era of Carías (1932–1949) brought a degree of domestic tranquillity as the practice of *continuismo*, or retention of power beyond the legal terms of office, came to be regarded as the only means of attaining political stability and reducing partisan conflict.

Tiburcio Carías Andino had run for the presidency twice before. The first time—in 1923—he failed to gain the required absolute majority by fewer than four thousand votes. Congress was unable to decide the three-way race, since Liberal party tactics obstructed any compromise, and Carías and his followers rose in armed revolt. The confusion was mediated by the United States. In February 1925, a compromise candidate, Miguel Paz Baraona, assumed the presidency. In 1928, the Liberal party defeated Carías by twelve thousand votes. The veteran politician of the National party, then president of the Congress, rejected rebellious pleas from some party stalwarts and respected the Liberal win. This decision, which gained Carías popularity and added stature, also gave him more time to consolidate his hold upon the National party. With the October 1932 elections, Carías finally won the needed majority by a convincing twenty thousand votes over the Liberal party led by Angel Zúñiga Huete.

The new president was a caudillo of the old school whose experience in Honduran revolts and governmental politics had begun during the early 1890s and whose influence was to be a factor in Honduran politics for another three decades. Don Tiburcio, standing over 6 feet, barrel-chested, with penetrating eyes and flaring white mustache, personified—perhaps too much—the archetypal image of a strong-man ruler. Carías definitely had control of his party, which he utilized to extend the authority of the state and manipulate elections. The Congress and the Supreme Court of Justice were filled with Nationalists loyal to the party leader and [in effect became] creatures of the chief executive. The press was squeezed to such a point that only an officially approved National party paper (La Epoca) survived. The jails held hundreds of political dissidents; many intellectuals, younger professionals, and Liberal party activists lived in exile throughout Central America, Mexico, and the United States.

Keenly aware of the difficulties had by Honduras at times of succession in power, the president convinced his Nationalist legislature to amend the Honduran constitution, changing his term of office from four to six years. Carías became the first Honduran chief executive to hold office more than one term. In 1939, officials were polled by Congress for their response to proposed changes in the constitution. The key provision was the extension of Carías's term as president until 1949, which was readily approved.

Although the era of Carías did bring a measure of peace and tranquillity to Honduras, it was achieved at the cost of supressed civil rights, restrictions on political activity, elimination of both national and local elections, and imposed authority. The regime did accomplish some positive goals, such as completion of the Pan American Highway through the southern portion of the country. Another 1,600 kilometers of unpaved feeder roads were constructed; schools were built in more isolated regions; Tegucigalpa gained a new airport. The central government and its growing bureaucracy filled new public buildings.

However, the rebellious spirit was not to be quelled so easily. Once Carías had violated the bounds of constitutionalism, Liberals led revolts and conducted subversive activities. Zúñiga Huete unleashed a constant but ineffective barrage of propaganda from his exile in Mexico. A now poverty-stricken Liberal party was driven underground, and its organization atrophied. The turning point for Carías came in 1944 when his fellow Central American dictators—Maximiliano Hernández in El Salvador and Guatemala's Jorge Ubico—tumbled from power. That same year there were demonstrations against the government in San Pedro Sula and Tegucigalpa. Police and military forces, firing on crowds of men, women, and children, killed several people in San Pedro Sula.

Under pressure from the United States, Carías pondered the feasibility of continuing in public office but realized that he could not seek another term without seriously threatening order and stability. The dictator settled upon Juan Manuel Gálvez Durón, his longtime minister of war and the "most honorable man he knew," as the National party candidate in the 1948 presidential elections. Gálvez and his running mate, Julio Lozano Díaz, won 80 percent of the October vote. It seemed a fitting climax to the era of Carías.

THE GÁLVEZ ERA, 1949–1954

The new chief of state assumed office with a more tolerant political perspective than his predecessor. Juan Manuel Gálvez traveled widely throughout Honduras by Jeep, on horseback, and on foot, often enhancing his image by slinging a coat over one shoulder as he talked with villagers and slum dwellers. The "shirt-sleeve" president, overly fond of cigars, diffused the tense political atmosphere by permitting exiles to return, releasing political prisoners, and allowing the Liberal party to reorganize itself under the leadership of Dr. José Ramón Villeda Morales. Three newspapers appeared to give *La Epoca* some competition.

Gálvez presided over the first in a series of international contacts that were to have a decided impact on Honduras. An International Monetary Fund (IMF) mission during 1950 recommended the establishment of the nation's first central bank (Central Bank of Honduras— BANTRAL) and the National Development Bank (BANADESA) and assisted in setting them up. Assistance was provided to organize the Faculty of Economics at the National University. The IMF mission's recommendations also led to the formation of the Superior Council of Economic Planning (CONSUPLANE) and the establishment of the Ministry of Economics and Commerce.[10] The Food and Agricultural Organization, a United Nations (UN) agency based in Rome, offered advice on forestry and agricultural extension programs. After 1954, the Inter-American Regional Organization of Workers (ORIT) worked with the nascent North Coast banana-worker unions through its subsidiary, the American Institute for Free Labor Development.

Also significant for Honduras was the impact of changed land-use patterns. Large-scale commercial agriculture expanded its holdings in response to revived world market prices for meat, cotton, and coffee. At the same time, new foreign investments helped to diversify the Honduran economic base. This "commercialization" of agriculture stimulated light industries like food processing, chemical production, and clothing manufactures.

In May 1954, the Gálvez administration was surprised by what turned out to be the country's only successful mass labor strike. Working-class organizations had appeared briefly during the early part of the 1920s, but labor activism was eradicated after 1932, and it was not until the 1954 strike that workers were able to sustain any movement toward establishing a viable labor movement. The turning point came when twenty-five thousand workers of the Tela Railroad Company (United Fruit) went on strike for higher wages, better working conditions, and ultimately for the right to organize and bargain collectively. The strike spread rapidly to the plantations of Standard Fruit, the mine at

El Mochito, and—gaining sympathy—to a host of processing industries in San Pedro Sula and Tegucigalpa. It was July before workers, companies, and the government were able to resolve the immediate conflict. Important advances for the labor movement were gained in organization and a sense of unity. Transcending these points in importance, elements of the Honduran working class had become a decisive political force in the realignment of such forces. This had been achieved independently of the traditional political parties.[11]

POLITICAL CHAOS, 1954–1956

Political change accelerated with the approach of elections in late 1954. The aging Carías, not content with his chosen successor's policies, demanded that the National party support him for the presidency. A split developed within the Nationalist ranks, and Abraham Williams Calderón ran against Carías as candidate of the dissident National Reformist Movement (MNR). Ramón Villeda Morales returned from political exile to campaign for the Liberals. The split among the Nationalists enabled the Liberals to win a plurality (48 percent) in the national elections, but without an absolute majority the election was thrown into the National Congress, where the distribution of seats favored the Nationalists and the MNR.

Political confusion was intensified when the Liberals were unable to command a quorum in the Congress. Seeing his chance, Vice-President Julio Lozano assumed all powers in accordance with provisions contained in the 1936 constitution. The new chief executive, sixty-nine years old when he gathered the powers of state into his hands, organized a Council of State to advise the president on matters of national policy. It included representatives from the three political parties plus three members appointed directly by the president.

The Lozano government's hold on legitimacy was tenuous; open opposition came from a variety of social groups. Existence of the Communist Party of Honduras (PCH), reorganized in 1954, provided the government an opportunity to associate dissident Liberals with "communism." Lozano decreed the PCH illegal and exiled many Liberal leaders during 1955. He organized his own political coalition, the National Unity party (PUN), and prepared to elect himself to a full presidential term. The Constituent Assembly elections of 7 October 1956 were the first in which Honduran women participated and that fact accounted for the turnout of over 400,000 voters. But with Liberals in exile and the Nationalists abstaining, election results that showed Lozano's coalition winning a 90 percent majority plunged the nation into even more turmoil.

Scarcely two weeks after the national elections, Julio Lozano was asked to turn power over to a military junta led by the military school commander, Gen. Roque J. Rodríguez. The junta's proclamation reasoned that "the Armed Forces of Honduras could not remain indifferent to the aspirations of the Honduran people who wished to return to a regime of order, of tranquility, and of law."[12] Elections were promised as soon as possible: Returning the country to constitutional rule was the only declared objective of the military. The fraudulent elections orchestrated by Lozano were judged invalid, and political amnesty was granted to political dissidents held in prison. The exiles gradually returned once again to Honduras.

2

The Setting:
Land and People

The context of land, climate, culture, and race often stimulates or moderates the course of a nation's history. In this sense, Honduran social, economic, and political development have been and remain significantly influenced by the country's geography and the characteristics of its population. Hondurans have coped with harsh physical conditions and inadequate infrastructures. For example, difficulties in communication and transport and the ruggedness of the topography hindered the growth of coffee as a competitive export during the nineteenth century. At the same time, the fertile but vacant and tropical lands of the North Coast invited extensive development by foreigners at the turn of the century.

As indicated in Chapter 1, internal isolation and minimal international contacts contributed to regionalism, reinforcing weak national identity and the evolution of caudillo politics. Foreign investors, meanwhile, exercised an unduly high degree of leverage upon national policy. Though distinctions among wealthy and poor, powerful and weak existed and though conflict, chaos, and instability marked the nation's political life, most Hondurans existed within a slightly bucolic and forgotten world. An appreciation of that world and the contemporary realities that Hondurans face allows a greater understanding of the problems and successes of Honduras during the last few decades, so it is appropriate at this point to review the physical and social characteristics of Honduras.

THE LAND

Honduras, located in the middle of the Central American isthmus, is bounded on the northwest by Guatemala, on the southwest by El Salvador, and on the south along the Rio Coco by Nicaragua (Figure 2.1). The Caribbean Sea lies north of Honduras and influences the country's orientation toward the Caribbean Basin. Extending nearly 650 kilometers from east to west and only 310 kilometers from north to

13

14

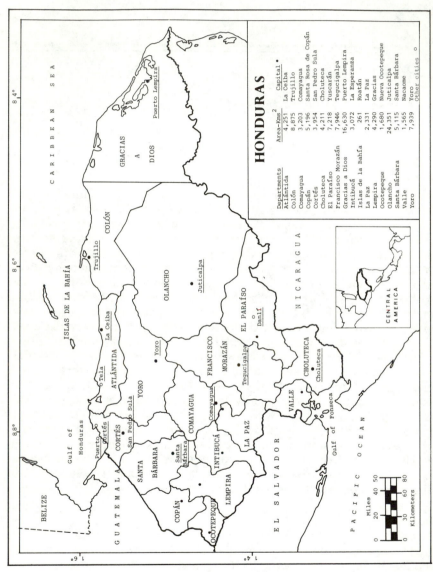

Figure 2.1   Map of Honduras

south, Honduras, with its 112,088 square kilometers, is about the size of Tennessee and follows Nicaragua as the second-largest country in Central America. Its population density as of 1980 was relatively low— thirty-two persons per square kilometer.

Regions

The country can be divided into three regions, or zones, according to geographic and socioeconomic characteristics. The *western region* is composed of those departments contiguous to El Salvador: Ocotepeque, Lempira, Intibucá, La Paz, and Valle. It also includes the departments of Santa Bárbara and Copán, which touch the Guatemalan frontier. This region constituted the southern limits of the pre-Columbian Quiché-Maya civilization. It generally has been the more densely populated area of Honduras, with lower average incomes and a greater incidence of illiteracy.

Farther south and east are the departments of Choluteca and El Paraíso, and in the central part of Honduras are found the departments of Francisco Morazán, Comayagua, and Yoro. Combined with the coastal departments of Cortés and Atlántida, these make up the *central region*— sometimes called the corridor of development. It is the zone that contains the most urban departments, has the most industry, receives greater amounts of public investment, and contains nearly three-quarters of the nation's economically active population.[1]

With its river valleys and coastal plains, the North Coast of Honduras has evolved since the 1900s as a dynamic center of agribusiness and industrial activity. (*North Coast* generally refers to Cortés, Atlántida, Colón, and occasionally portions of Yoro.) The focal point of this subregion is San Pedro Sula, the second-largest, but busiest, city in Honduras. It is situated in the Ulua River valley nearly 60 kilometers from the Caribbean port of Puerto Cortés.

Extending south from San Pedro Sula and dividing Honduras from north to south is a transisthmian depression, in effect a series of interconnected river valleys and interior highland basins. It passes through the so-called development corridor from the Ulua Valley to Lake Yoyoa at an altitude of 600 meters, on to Comayagua, goes past the capital city of Tegucigalpa, and ends at the Gulf of Fonseca. Through this transverse valley the highway from San Pedro Sula runs 258 kilometers to Tegucigalpa and then south 92 kilometers to San Lorenzo, a major new port city.

The least populated and most isolated parts of Honduras make up the *eastern region* of Olancho, Colón, and Gracias a Dios. Covered with hardwood and pine forests and containing undeveloped mineral resources, the zone is primarily agrarian and pastoral, with few roads or major population centers. At the same time, Olancho and Gracias a Dios represent over a third of Honduran territory and include most of the nation's state-owned lands.

Mountains

Unlike the rest of Central America, Honduras is a land without active volcanoes. Rather its terrain is primarily a confusing jumble of intersecting mountain ranges covering nearly two-thirds of the country. The remaining territory is composed of coastal plains, inland river valleys, and several higher-elevation intermontane basins.

The mountains are divided roughly into three areas; the highest and most extensive is the southwestern highlands along the 343-kilometer border with El Salvador. The highest point, Montaña de Celaque, rises to 2,850 meters near Gracias, the provincial capital of Lempira. The lower central highlands average between 1,500 and 2,100 meters in the departments of Comayagua and Francisco Morazán. The mountains extend eastward to the Nicaraguan border and south into the departments of Valle and Choluteca. Only a narrow 40-kilometer-wide strip remains along the Pacific coast. Through this dry, hot, and sparse lowland passes the Pan-American Highway. For 145 kilometers, the Pacific coastline circles the Gulf of Fonseca. The largest of the islands in the gulf is Sacate Grande. The former port city of Amapala is on El Tigre island.

A third mountain region is the north-central highlands of Yoro, Olancho, and Colón. These ranges intersect the northern coast of Honduras diagonally along a southwest-northeast axis. The Cordillera of Nombre de Dios overlooks the city of La Ceiba and rises to 2,435 meters scarcely 20 kilometers from the sea. Behind these ranges are the important valleys of the Aguán, Sico, and Paulaya rivers. Farther east, the mountains terminate in a flat plain that extends into Nicaragua. These thinly settled tropical lowlands of Gracias a Dios are known as the Mosquitia.

Bay Islands

Distinct in geography and culture is the department of Islas de la Bahía (Bay Islands), just off the northern coast near La Ceiba. There are three main islands—Roatán, Guanaja, and Utila—along with several smaller islands and cays. One hundred and seventy miles northeast of the Bay Islands are the Swan Islands which have always been claimed by Honduras. Through a treaty ratified in 1972, they were ceded by the United States to Honduras.

Climate and Natural Resources

Climate in Honduras varies according to local topography and elevation. The coastal plains and river valleys are tropical, with higher levels of rainfall along the North Coast, especially in the Mosquitia region. The south coast receives less rainfall, since the predominant winds come from the north. A wet season continues from May until October with precipitation ranging from 1,000 millimeters at Tegucigalpa to over 3,000 at Tela on the northern coast. Temperatures vary with altitude—the torrid, humid lowlands average around 26 degrees cen-

Pine forests covering much of upland Honduras are a substantial natural resource for the country.

tigrade. Mountain elevations are moderate to cool, with the interior valley temperatures becoming quite warm during dry-season days. Tegucigalpa averages a comfortable 20 degrees centigrade.

Nearly half the mountain terrain is covered with extensive hardwood and pine forests. The department of Gracias a Dios supports mangrove thickets along swampy shorelines, and there are Caribbean pines at higher elevations. Mahogany, rosewood, Spanish cedar, and balsa are found throughout the warmer humid regions. The most widespread forest consists of the pines found on the western slopes and covering much of Olancho department. Long recognized as a principal resource, the pine forests figure prominently in future development plans.

Other natural resources include gold, silver, zinc, lead, iron ore, and other metalliferous ores. Marble, gypsum, and limestone are actively mined in the north-central region. There are proven reserves of some 15 million metric tons of lignite in western Honduras. Reports of potential hydrocarbon deposits and petroleum reserves are periodically leaked to

The highland valleys are key to Honduran agricultural production.

the press; though the information is not clear, transnational oil companies
have been conducting various explorations under contract from the
government. For now, Honduras is totally dependent for its petroleum
supply on imports from Venezuela and Mexico.[2]

Despite the dominance of agriculture in the national economy, the
soils are relatively infertile. The country is not covered with the layer
of volcanic ash found in the other republics of the region, since the
axis of the Central American volcanoes skirts the southern boundaries
of Honduras. Arable lands, from 30 to 33 percent of the national territory,
are located along the coasts, in river valleys, and on the flat portions
of the intermontane basins.

Accessibility

The development of Honduras has been affected by rugged topography and the relative isolation of extensive portions of the country.
Some areas are still accessible only on foot or by muleback. Difficulties
in reaching market centers have kept some regions minimally populated,
especially the eastern zone departments of Olancho, parts of Colón,
and Gracias a Dios. It was not until 1970 that the major highway
between Tegucigalpa and the North Coast industrial center of San Pedro
Sula became an all-weather paved road.

By the 1980s, Honduras could count nearly 13,500 kilometers of
roads and highways, with about two-thirds considered all weather.

Expressway construction has been started in and around the Central District in accordance with a master transportation plan; traffic from the north eventually will be routed through the environs of Tegucigalpa, connecting with a redesigned Carretera del Sur. This route emerges more and more as a principal trade channel between northern and southern coasts, linking the former port of Amapala and the new port of San Lorenzo on the Gulf of Fonseca with the nation's most active maritime city of Puerto Cortés. Container shipping is increasing in volume and importance along this route. Although not competitive with the Panama Canal, its potential as an alternative has been considered by past governments.

Prior to 1974, Honduras owned a minor portion of its railways, which were operated by the National Railroad of Honduras (FNH). The remaining lines were controlled by Standard Fruit, headquartered in La Ceiba, and the Tela Railroad Company, a subsidiary of United Fruit (now United Brands). The rail lines were designed to accommodate the transportation of supplies needed by the fruit industry and shipment of its produce to wharves located in Trujillo, La Ceiba, Tela, and Puerto Cortés. As a result, the routes are confined to the North Coast region. At the height of the 1975 United Brands bribery scandal, the government nationalized the fruit-company lines. The FNH now operates almost 1,000 kilometers of railroads hauling freight and passengers. There is no line to Tegucigalpa, making it the only capital city in Central America without rail service.

THE PEOPLE

Spanish settlers gravitated to the cooler and more comfortable interior highland basins. The native inhabitants of what is now Honduras were concentrated in the western portion of the country; the northern and northeastern lowlands were basically uninhabited until the latter part of the nineteenth century. In general terms, this remains true: The seven departments touching the Salvadoran and Guatemalan borders, with one-fifth of the national territory, contain one-fifth of the country's total population (forty-two persons per square kilometer). The more urban, central-corridor departments, with 35 percent of the territory, are increasing in population by migration from the western zone and parts of Olancho. The urban concentrations of Tegucigalpa and San Pedro Sula result in a higher average density of fifty-nine people per square kilometer.

The eastern part of Honduras in many respects remains a frontier. The province of Olancho, larger than the whole country of El Salvador, counts eight persons per square kilometer. The even more remote Gracias a Dios accounts for less than 1 percent of the total population or fewer than two people per square kilometer. The migratory trend from west to east will continue as available lands, the forests, and untapped mineral

The Peatonal: Tegucigalpa's main street was turned into a pedestrian walkway during the late 1970s.

A *barrio*, or neighborhood, of rapidly growing Tegucigalpa.

resources of the eastern zone are gradually exploited. The national population was estimated at 3.8 million in 1983, but with current growth rates (3.25–3.5 percent), the population is expected to double before the year 2000 (Table 2.1).[3]

Poverty

The Honduran legacy of being the poorest in Central America is reflected in its national social statistics. Often referred to as a country of the seventies, it might now be known as a nation of the sixties. It is 63 percent rural; about 60 percent of the economically active population (EAP) works in agriculture, mining, forestry, or fishing; only 60 percent of the population is considered functionally literate (although the percentage is increasing). During the latter part of the 1970s, with almost half of all Hondurans under fifteen years of age, a youthful demographic profile posed problems of providing basic services and developing adequate employment opportunities. Unemployment averaged around 9 percent of the economically active population in 1978; underemployment was estimated at around 37 percent.[4] These figures grew worse during the economic decline of the early 1980s, as almost three-fifths of the EAP were either out of work or surviving with partial employment.

It has been pointed out that four-fifths of all Hondurans could be considered to live under conditions of poverty. Using a "nutritionally-at-risk" standard, a 1978 agricultural assessment survey estimated that

TABLE 2.1
Social and Economic Indicators for Honduras, 1961, 1974, 1980s

	1961	1974	1980s
Population	1,884,765	2,656,948[a]	3,594,700[b]
Annual Rate of Population Growth	2.95%	3.34%	3.47%
Population Density[c] (112,088 sq. kms.)	16.8	23.6	32.1
Literacy Rate	47.3%	57.1%	59.5%
Urban Population	23.2%	31.4%	36.8% (1981)
Economically Active Population (EAP)	568,000	792,000	1,166,500 (1982)
Gross Domestic Product (GDP) Per Capita (1980 dollars)	$469	$541	$616 (1981)
External Public Debt[d]	$23 (1960)	$276	$1,600 (1982)
GDP by Sector[e]			
Agriculture	37%	34%	31%
Industry	19	23	26
Services	44	43	43
EAP by Sector[e]			
Agriculture	70%	62%	60%
Industry	11	15	16
Services	19	23	24

Sources: Honduran census data; Inter-American Development Bank (IDB), World Bank, Central Bank of Honduras, and Latin American Demographic Center (CELADE).

[a] IDB estimate; CELADE estimate was 2,897,500.

[b] CELADE estimate; IDB estimate was 3,691,000. Estimates for 1983 range from 3.8 to 4.1 million.

[c] People per square kilometer

[d] Millions of dollars

[e] Agriculture includes forestry, hunting, and fishing; industry includes mining, manufacturing, construction, electricity, gas and water; services includes all other activities.

64 percent of the rural population was poor.[5] Poverty in this case included those families (average size of 6.2) unable to purchase or acquire minimum dietary needs. In 1977 prices this required an average annual per capita income of $260 ($300 urban, $220 rural). Though urban incomes are higher, costs are greater. In any case, few of the urban poor have incomes greater than the indicated standard.

Street vendors offer a variety of wares and services.

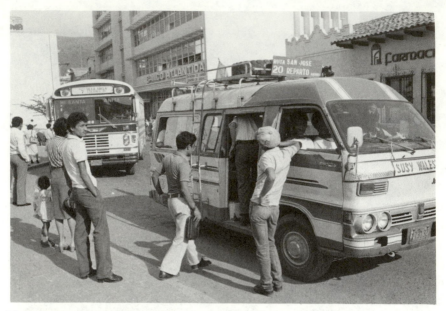

The most popular transportation in the capital city is the *busito*.

Urban-Rural Differences

The social and economic aspects of poverty are exacerbated by differences between urban centers and rural areas. Rural fertility rates are almost double those of the urban areas, and the proportion of population under fifteen years is greater in rural areas. Inequalities of income distribution are more severe, and the extent of illiteracy is two and a half times higher in the rural sector. As of 1978, life expectancy was ten years less than in the cities, or fifty versus sixty-one years; infant mortality rates were half again higher. Much of the Honduran population experiences caloric deficits, but among rural children under five years the figure rises to 90 percent.

Access to services and resources varies dramatically in both urban and rural areas. Education, health, and housing conditions differ among families depending on the amount of resources they are able to acquire or their success in qualifying for governmental services and assistance: for example, loans, credit, technical advice, new schools, or neighborhood health clinics. Generally, services are more available in the urban zones. Government policy addresses the more evident and pressing issues first. To extend services more evenly would tax both available resources and administrative capacity. Despite miserable environmental conditions found in the cities (malnutrition, inadequate housing, lack of amenities such as running water and sewerage), life is viewed as more dynamic and is seen to hold in some degree more opportunities for upward mobility.

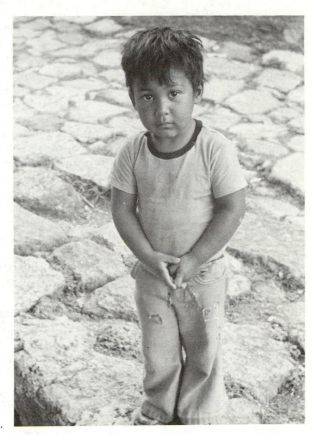

A young Honduran.

Ethnic and Racial Characteristics

Whereas quality of life and opportunities vary widely between urban and rural sectors in Honduras, the ethnic and racial composition of the society is much more homogeneous. The Spanish colonizers encountered a sparse and scattered native population; except for the western border region, Honduras remained outside the Mesoamerican aboriginal culture area. New arrivals intermarried easily with native inhabitants, and Hondurans are racially mixed.

Nearly 90 percent are considered *mestizo,* generally the blending of Spanish and Indian racial characteristics. Similarly, the society conforms almost entirely to what is termed the *ladino* culture in manners of dress, daily living patterns, language, and values. The term *ladino* specifically refers to the cultural blend of Hispanic and indigenous elements, with European forms, customs, and language dominating. Persons of various racial backgrounds and racial mixtures are considered to be ladino when they have adopted the dominant ladino patterns and values. *Mestizo* and *ladino* are often interchangeable terms. In the context of Central American culture, Honduras is considered a mestizo country along with El Salvador, Nicaragua, and Panama; Costa Rica is more "European" and Guatemala predominately "Indian" in racial and cultural composition. From this perspective, the society and culture of Honduras are derived primarily from its Hispanic heritage, with an admixture of indigenous forms. More recently, during the late nineteenth century and throughout the twentieth century, the influence of the United States—economic, political, cultural—has become an important factor in Honduran national development. Even so, due to the country's historical and physical isolation and its relatively low level of urbanization, much of Honduran society reflects the traditional values of a real peasant culture. Personalism, with its implications for self-identity and relations with others, and the hierarchical nature of authority patterns that affect relationships among socioeconomic classes are combined with a pervading sense of fatalism drawn from the Hispanic heritage, Catholicism, and the rigors of subsistence agriculture.

The remaining nonmestizo 10 percent of the population is ethnically and racially distributed among several Indian cultures, a small black population, and Caucasians. Constituting about 7 percent of the nation, the Indians of Honduras live mostly in the departments of Lempira, Intibucá, and La Paz.[6] This area is inhabited by the descendants of the Lenca culture. Assimilation and erosion of the remaining indigenous culture proceed, yet these areas are still distinctive in that landholding patterns are more communal than in other parts of the country. Isolated groups of Indians are found in Santa Bárbara, Copán, and El Paraíso. The Jicaque have gradually retreated from the coastal zones into the Montaña de la Flor region of Yoro department. The riverine Paya, Sumu, and Miskitos make their home in the far northeastern lowlands of Gracias a Dios and the isolated forests of eastern Olancho and Colón.

Though the black population is small, there are two distinctive groups. The first to arrive were the black Caribs commonly referred to as *morenos*, descendants of Negro-Indians marooned by the British in 1797 on the Bay Islands. The Caribs later abandoned the islands to the Spanish and settled on the mainland at Trujillo. Gradually they have migrated westward, living in several coastal villages.[7] The moreno communities are often trilingual, speaking Carib with Spanish and English as second and third languages. Black Caribs have kept close to the sea, often work on the docks, and play prominent roles in the transportation phase of the banana industry.

The expansion of the banana-plantation economy developed a need for labor that led to the importation of Antillean Negro workers from British Honduras (now Belize), the Cayman Islands, and Jamaica. This second Negro population lives close to the northern coast and in the Bay Islands. The islands are also home to the distinctive but minuscule Antillean white society. These English-speaking peoples migrated during the 1830s, again primarily from Belize, the Caymans, Jamaica, and other islands of the Greater and Lesser Antilles.

Another assimilated yet distinguishable ethnic group is that of the descendants of eastern Mediterranean immigrants who arrived between 1900 and 1910, collectively known as *los arabes* (the Arabs). Many autochthonous Hondurans describe this community in sinister terms of clannishness and opportunism. The original immigrants came to Honduras with little except their ambition and commercial heritage, and they quickly took advantage of the vacuum within the private sector that developed alongside the plantation agriculture on the North Coast. Cultural barriers erected previously by both the Levantine ethnics and Honduran society have dissipated, as intermarriage is common and Spanish is clearly the native language of third and fourth generations.

Catholicism

The Spanish conquistadores introduced Catholicism during their exploits in the Americas, and it remains the dominant religion in Latin America. It is estimated that nearly 90 percent of all Hondurans are nominally Catholic. The remainder follow more indigenous religious forms or some combination of Catholicism and folklore. Increasing numbers have been converted or influenced by Protestant missionaries. The Catholic church was first established in Honduras by 1521 and later developed by the Franciscan order. Historically a poor church, it has controlled little real estate or acquired few alternate sources of income.[8] With Honduran independence, the church suffered a decline in its influence as tithes were reduced or eliminated and monastic orders were dissolved. After 1880, Liberal reforms further restricted privileges, legally separated church and state, and revoked the Concordat with the Vatican.

The Catholic church is organized into the archdiocese of Tegucigalpa, dioceses in Santa Rosa de Copán, San Pedro Sula, and Comayagua, and prelatures in Olancho and Choluteca. Divided into over one hundred parishes, many priests are foreign born, and generally there is a shortage of clerical personnel. Monastic orders are allowed once again, and the government provides some subsidies to religious denominations and supports religious instruction in public schools.

Baptism, marriage, novenas, and *posadas* are part of the daily life of most Hondurans. Two aspects that bear mention are the various pilgrimages, mostly of local importance, and town fiestas. The pilgrimage and shrine of national importance is located outside Tegucigalpa near the Autonomous National University of Honduras (UNAH) in the village (*aldea*) of Suyapa. The fiesta of Our Lady of Suyapa, the patron saint of Honduras, is celebrated on February third. Local fiestas are numerous as each town celebrates its patron saint's day annually. Planning, fund raising, and the celebrations themselves involve local officials, citizen groups, and parish priests. In a broader sense, the religious aspects of fiestas combine with the anticipation of recreation and in some cases

The eighteenth-century cathedral in Tegucigalpa.

an economic boost from returning relatives and visiting tourists. The annual fair at La Ceiba features a beauty contest, outdoor amusement rides, and a seaside tent where games of chance attract a noisy but optimistic crowd.

Though Catholicism predominates in Honduras, the Bay Islands and other areas on the North Coast include significant strongholds of Protestants. The Methodist church was first established on the islands in 1859. Other Protestant and evangelical groups were introduced during the early part of the century. The Evangelical and Reformed church established a boarding school in San Pedro Sula; other denominations followed suit in maintaining elementary and secondary schools as well as small health-care centers. Active proselytization continued into the late 1960s. Though Protestants have constituted a distinct minority, the positive image derived from their array of community services presented an ideological challenge to a semidormant Catholic church.[9] Other religious influences are a scattering of original Indian practices and some African traditions that remain among the black populations.

The Catholic church has not had a significant political or social impact in Honduras. The church's poverty and shortage of priests have hindered its ability to extend and retain its presence in the country's isolated rural areas. On the other hand, Catholicism itself forms part of the Honduran value structure and is observed in the respect for the sacraments, patron saints, and national holidays. Also, religious values and sentiment have been uncovered and stimulated by several Protestant sects. In part, it was the latter activity that prompted the Catholic church to launch a religious revival campaign during the late 1950s. Its objective was to revitalize the church's rural parish bases. The program—integrating religious, community development, and educational aspects—indirectly contributed to the rise of an active, organized peasant movement during the 1960s and 1970s (see Chapter 6).

The Honduran Catholic church today promotes moral and social justice. Through its infrequent but dramatic and forthright pastoral letters, it urges both government and the country's leadership to promote reforms and respect for human rights. It condemns violence as a legitimate form of social change. The church's political role has not followed the example of the church in El Salvador nor that of the embattled church in Nicaragua. Principally, this is because the dynamics of Honduran culture, social development, and politics have been distinct. The church has yet to be forced into making a final choice between radical reformism and strict adherence to the status quo.

Class Structure

Racial and ethnic differences are not overly important for purposes of identification or social status. For the most part a mestizo country, there is a great deal of borrowing from both ladino and Indian cultural backgrounds. Of the estimated 3.8 million inhabitants of Honduras, over 60 percent work and live in rural areas. And it is this urban-rural division that appears to be a major determinant of the social structure. This dichotomous culture originated as the Spanish imposed their values upon what remained of the Indian societies. The elites concentrated themselves in provincial capitals and the larger urban settlements, since rural living was regarded as inferior in status as well as in its living standards. Likewise, political privilege and the monopoly on literacy have been largely aspects of urban life. The literate society and the contemporary urban-technical sectors have resisted integrating the rural masses into the broader social and economic life of the nation. With industrial expansion after World War II, the urban sector further consolidated its position and increased its share of the new wealth, as it was the only element readily capable of participating in and benefiting from new economic growth.[10]

The peasant traditionally has been relegated to the fringes of the economy, and the urban elites have utilized industrial growth as another

Hillside settlements of the capital city are often without utilities and other urban services.

means of maintaining their position of political control. Rural elites began to rationalize their use of land during the late 1950s and early 1960s. The traditional patron-client relationship between rural landlord and rural masses became less important and the peasantry, left more and more to its own resources, became for a time even more isolated.

A prominent characteristic of the Honduran class structure is the extent to which the lower classes have been only marginally incorporated into national life. Four-fifths of the rural lower classes consist of traditional farmers whose production is near or at subsistence levels or landless farmers who squat on private or government lands, hire out as day laborers, or survive by sharecropping. The urban lower classes are expanding primarily as a result of migration from countryside and from small towns to the cities. Those who live in the hillside slums of Tegucigalpa and other poor neighborhoods are ill housed, without services, and make up the bulk of the unemployed. All indications are that the lower classes account for nearly two-thirds of the Honduran

Tegucigalpa's valley viewed from Colonia Miraflores.

population. They are mostly rural, have high rates of illiteracy, and live at subsistence levels.

Almost 60 percent of the labor force works in agriculture, including landowners as well as plantation workers. The plantation laborers, rather than being part of the lower classes, are considered part of the working class along with manufacturing and industrial workers. The banana workers are the largest segment of organized labor. Union members, although a small proportion of the national labor force, economically and politically occupy a stronger position, since they usually qualify for social-security provisions and other fringe benefits and earn a wage that is two to three times that of the average worker.

The urban-based middle classes include government employees, shopkeepers, service personnel, office workers, school teachers, and younger professionals. The proportion of middle sectors in Honduran society increased after 1950 along with expanding industrial capacity and opportunities for higher education. It has been the middle classes that have benefited most from training programs and scholarships. And it is they who have occupied the suburban housing developments, or *colonias*, that now surround the center of Tegucigalpa and other urban centers.[11]

Traditional landowning families make up the upper classes along with the industrial and financial entrepreneurs of more recent years. It is from these upper socioeconomic groups that most high-level governmental posts are filled. Some observers divide the upper stratum into

A view from Parque
Leona in Tegucigalpa.

two levels, with the more wealthy, cosmopolitan elite living in the capital
and San Pedro Sula. Old-line local elites, sometimes referred to as *la
primera*, reside in departmental capitals and retain influence derived
from possession of property, past wealth, or long-established respect
for family lines.[12]

Even though the class structure follows the archetypal Latin American pattern of small urban elite, nascent middle and working classes,
and large rural peasantry, Honduras never has been able to produce
and maintain a solid landowning aristocracy as in other Central and
South American countries. Although large landowners are economically
and politically powerful, there is another important difference in the
Honduran class structure. Despite the urban-rural dichotomy, the lower
classes, working class, and upper class have linkages or interests in both
the urban and rural sectors. In the case of the upper class(es), investments
are in different economic activities. Labor organizations facilitate communication among urban workers, organized agricultural laborers, and

numerous peasant organizations. The essential bifurcation of the Honduran society remains, but—with economic and social differentiation—the emerging class structure has begun to cut across economic sectors and overlap the urban-rural division.

Migration

The profile of Honduran social and economic structures has been stimulated and shaped by patterns of migration and urbanization. Along with commercial exports, entry into the Central American Common Market, and a gradual diversification of the industrial sector, two markets for agricultural products were created after World War II—an international demand for meat and cotton and the food needs of expanding urban centers. Viewing their resources in more rational economic terms, large landholders began to cultivate lands that were formerly leased or neglected. At times the expansion occurred onto national or communal (*ejidal*) lands. The impact upon the rural population was immediate and evident, as peasants were evicted or prohibited from cultivating lands that they had utilized freely in prior years.

Changing rural conditions added to the flow of people toward Honduran cities and into regions where economic opportunities were more numerous or where land was available. Most of the available land was located in the north-central and eastern regions of the country. Agribusiness and industrial expansion along the North Coast attracted people in search of work, opportunities for education, and other benefits that rarely existed in the Honduran countryside.

With slight differences between the 1950–1961 and 1961–1974 intercensal periods, the migration pattern has been from western Honduras toward the north and east. It also occurs in phases: rural to urban, urban to urban.[13] Regions of the highest outmigration are the southwestern highland departments along the border with El Salvador. Other zones of "expulsion" are the departments of Olancho, Valle, Choluteca, and El Paraíso. The department of Francisco Morazán receives newcomers from the center of the country, the western zone, and from the south. Santa Bárbara and Copán receive population from the western departments. Subsequent migration is toward Cortés, Atlántida, Colón, and Yoro. The North Coast also gains population from Tegucigalpa, Comayagua, and Olancho. This latter phase is primarily urban-to-urban movement, but there is also an exodus from parts of the coastal zone as people gravitate back to the capital city or push on to less populated areas of Colón and Gracias a Dios. The North Coast departments have persistently been areas of "attraction" since the 1900s. With the evolution of the banana-export industry, and then industrial expansion, the need for available labor rose steadily. In effect, the national migration patterns emerged between poles of attraction and expulsion; the former were focal points for capitalistic development, whereas the latter had higher land-to-population ratios and were oriented to subsistence agriculture.

Migration is a prime contributor to urban growth. Urban migration flows proportionately include more women, since men tend to migrate to areas of agricultural employment or to regions where land is likely to be available. Most who migrate are less than twenty-five years old. This implies that areas of emigration are losing a good share of their more productive people. Honduras is distinct from other countries in Central America as it does not have an overly dominant primate city. In 1980, Tegucigalpa represented only 42 percent of the nation's urban population, the lowest proportion for any capital city in the region. Comparatively, San José accounted for 65 percent of Costa Rica's urban populace, and Guatemala City and its environs contained nearly three-quarters of that nation's urban population.[14] The capital of Honduras also competes with the faster-growing industrial and commercial center of San Pedro Sula. Other cities such as Puerto Cortés, La Ceiba, El Progreso, and Choluteca range between thirty-five and fifty-five thousand in population and continue to attract new residents.

3

Modernization and
New Elites, 1956–1972

The October 1956 coup marked the entry of a refurbished, professionalized military into Honduran politics. One de facto government had been replaced by another, but this time with obvious involvement of the armed forces. Not so clear were the reasons—beyond the simple threat to domestic peace. Certainly, resistance to Pres. Julio Lozano's increasingly harsh rule had been spreading. There were also indications that Lozano had been dragging his feet on Honduran entry into the Central American Common Market, and it appeared that both Honduran and foreign business interests were not averse to a change in the presidency.[1] Factions in the traditional political parties also had much to gain with Lozano absent, and it seemed unlikely that the armed forces would have acted totally on their own initiative at this point in Honduran history.

At the same time, evolution of a military institutional identity had been developing and was a new aspect within Honduran politics. The military was no longer the private army of a strong political leader, but rather was "an organic part of the State." Loyalty had momentarily transcended personalism: Constitutionality and country were now more important. Therefore, civil violence or the threat of civil war became concerns of the armed forces when either threatened the state or the military's institutional integrity.

In July 1957, General Rodríguez was forced out of the junta by military members of the cabinet. Lt. Col. Oswaldo López Arellano had accused the general of "playing politics." A few months later, López Arellano became a member of the junta without relinquishing his post as minister of defense.

Elections for a Constituent Assembly had been called for 21 September 1957, and more than 500,000 had registered to vote. Just before election day, regular military personnel were assigned to replace local *comandantes*—traditional police units used to maintain order before

TABLE 3.1
Chief Executives and Changes of Government in Honduras, 1932–1982

Chief Executive	Type of Change	Date of Change
Tiburcio Carías Andino PNH* (1933–1949)	Elections New Constitution Term extended	30 October 1932 1936 1939
Juan Manuel Gálvez PNH (1949–1954)	Elections	11 October 1948
Julio Lozano Díaz PNH (1954–1956)	Elections Elections	10 October 1954 7 October 1956
Military Triumvirate (1956–1957)	Coup	21 October 1956
Ramón Villeda Morales PLH* (1957–1963)	Elections	21 September 1957
Col. Oswaldo López Arellano (1963–1965)	Coup	3 October 1963
Gen. Oswaldo López Arellano PNH (1965–1971)	Elections	12 February 1965
Ramón Ernesto Cruz PNH (1971–1972)	Elections	28 March 1971
Gen. Oswaldo López Arellano (1972–1975)	Coup	4 December 1972
Gen. Juan Alberto Melgar Castro (1975–1978)	Internal Coup	22 April 1975
Gen. Policarpo Paz García (1978–1982)	Internal Coup	7 August 1978
Roberto Suazo Córdova PLH (1982–)	Elections	29 November 1981

*
PNH = National Party of Honduras; PLH = Liberal Party of Honduras

the development of a modern military. The dispersion of regular troops was to insure smooth, honest elections, although at this point the military was still not fully able to challenge the strongest local political bosses.

The Liberals and their returned leader, Ramón Villeda Morales, won every department, capturing 62 percent of the total vote (Table 3.1). The Nationalists were still split with the *cariistas* (Carías supporters) and the *reformistas* (followers of the MNR) sharing the remaining votes (Table 3.2). The victory left the Liberals fully in control of the Constituent Assembly. The next step was the choice of a new president and approval of a new constitution. With some collaboration between the Liberal

TABLE 3.2
National Elections in Honduras, 1954–1981

Year	Liberal Party	National Party	Third Parties[a]	Total Voters[b]	Registered Voters
1954	122,312 (47.9%)[c]	79,648 (31.2%)[c]	53,241 (20.9%)[c]	255,231	*
1956[d]	41,724 (10.1%)	2,003 (0.5%)	370,318 (89.4%)	414,045	*
1957[d]	209,109 (61.5%)	101,274 (29.8%)	29,489 (8.7%)	339,872 (65.1%)[e]	522,359
1965[d]	272,062 (44.2%)	335,726 (49.3%)	---	614,696 (75.4%)	815,261
1971	269,989 (44.4%)	299,807 (49.3%)	---	608,342 (67.5%)	900,658
1980[d]	495,768 (49.4%)	423,642 (42.2%)	35,044 (3.5%)	1,003,470 (81.3%)	1,233,756
1981	636,392 (52.4%)	491,089 (40.4%)	48,582 (4.0%)	1,214,735 (80.7%)	1,504,658

Sources: 1954, El Cronista (20 October 1954); 1956, Anderson in Needler; 1957, El Día (23 September 1957); 1965, 1971, Consejo Nacional de Elecciones; 1980, 1981, Tribunal Nacional de Elecciones.

*Number of registered voters not available for 1954 and 1956.

[a]The third parties were: 1954, MNR; 1956, PUN; 1957, MNR; 1980, PINU; 1981, PINU and PDCH.

[b]Totals include blank and null ballots.

[c]Percentage of total voters

[d]Constituent Assembly elections

[e]Percentage of registered voters

party leader and military commanders, indirect elections were accepted. The assembly converted itself into the National Congress while confirming the appointment of Villeda Morales as president of the republic.

THE LIBERAL INTERLUDE, 1957–1963

After twenty-five years, the PLH had regained the presidency and control over the congress. The first years of the Villeda administration paralleled changes introduced during the 1876 Liberal reform period. The Development Law of 1958 (Ley de Fomento) provided tax relief and investment guarantees to both domestic and foreign capital. The same year, a Social Security Law was enacted and the Honduran Institute for Social Security (IHSS) was set up to administer the program. With assistance from the American Institute for Free Labor Development, a modern labor code was drafted guaranteeing unions the right to organize and bargain collectively. Another milestone was reached with the approval of an Agrarian Reform Law in 1962.

In the midst of these positive accomplishments, frequent crises erupted to keep the Liberal government slightly off balance. The president devoted personal attention to a 1958 banana-worker strike; he defended charges that his administration leaned toward "communism"; he went to Monjarás in Choluteca to resolve an illegal land occupation by peasant groups. The victory of Fidel Castro in Cuba stimulated debate and organizing among peasants and workers. In response to the Cuban revolution, the United States sponsored the Alliance for Progress and urged basic reforms and government programs in housing, health, and education. At the same time, the Catholic church was in the process of revitalizing its rural bases through literacy programs, religious revivals, and community development projects.

The Villeda government was buffeted in the other direction by conservative pressures. Large landowners and the fruit companies fought the agrarian reform and other social measures. It was surmised that the surviving dictators in the Caribbean Basin—Trujillo in the Dominican Republic and Somoza in neighboring Nicaragua—supported efforts to overturn the Honduran government. Internally, National party factions backed a perennially unhappy, rebellious Col. Armando Velásquez Cerrato, who had missed out in the 1956 elections. Supported by units of the fourth military zone in Comayagua and civilian opponents of the government, he led divisions of the National Police in a series of revolts for several months during 1959. The culmination came in July when armed civilians supportive of the regime and the Presidential Guard fended off attacks on the Presidential Palace. Colonel Velásquez was allowed asylum at the suggestion of the armed forces, which had intervened only after the conflict had been clarified militarily.[2]

It was this event that convinced Villeda Morales of the need to reorganize his security forces. The National Police had evolved under National party auspices and were attached to the Ministry of Defense. The minister, Col. Oswaldo López Arellano, was also head of the armed forces and ostensibly had authority over all security forces in the country. After their complicity in the armed revolts, the National Police were dissolved, and a Civil Guard of nearly two thousand was organized under the authority of the Ministry of Government and Justice. The reaction of the military was negative, since the guard was perceived as a potential threat to institutional autonomy of the armed forces.

According to the 1957 constitution, the head of the armed forces was the highest military authority. The National Congress by majority vote filled the position from a list submitted by the Superior Council of National Defense. The armed forces leader in turn selected and assigned the various zone commanders. Article 319 of the constitution also stated that "orders given by the President of the Republic to the Armed Forces through its Head, must be respected. Whenever any difference arises it should be submitted to the Congress for its consideration and resolution of the issue by majority vote. This decision will be definitive and must be obeyed."[3]

The creation of the Civil Guard numbered the days left for the Liberals' "Second Republic." The political environment of attacks by the left—criticizing Villeda Morales for not favoring the working classes enough—and accusations of communist infiltration by the right took its toll upon the administration. Villeda Morales backed away, gradually disarming the Civil Guard, but this failed to prevent clashes between guard and military units. Whether sought purposely or not, the conflicts spread anxiety and distrust. The cycle of tension and divisiveness had returned, and the outlook for the 1963 elections was not optimistic.

The president of the republic pondered whom he might support as Liberal party candidate. It would preferably be someone who would return the favor in 1969 and the next presidential elections. Modesto Rodas Alvarado, a protégé of Angel Zúñiga Huete, the Liberal party leader during the reign of Carías, was among the most popular of several candidates mentioned in party circles. Not a favorite of Villeda Morales, Rodas did not depend upon his patron or the president to gain his party's favor. Instead "he went to small villages, the lowlands, into humble shacks, and the far corners of the land spreading his raucous message of vengeance and rage for those who opposed the party in power. Waving the flag, he amassed great popularity."[4] Using the powers of his office, President Villeda Morales tried to dictate his party's choice, but Rodas Alvarado easily unified the Liberals around his candidacy.

A similar situation evolved within the National party when the *cariista* faction supported Gen. Tiburcio Carías, by then seventy-eight years old. The aging caudillo insisted that his son Gonzalo be named as the Nationalist candidate, but the majority favored the moderate and statesmanlike Juan Manuel Gálvez. The National party finally compromised by choosing Dr. Ramón Ernesto Cruz Uclés, a longtime Nationalist and well-known jurist. He was a colorless campaigner in comparison with the fiery Rodas, who stumped the country urging more social reforms and advocating revision of Article 319 of the 1957 constitution that lent the military its autonomous status.

Ten days before the scheduled elections, another Honduran president was forced to leave office before the end of his term. On 3 October 1963, the birthday of Honduran hero Francisco Morazán, Colonel López Arellano seized all powers of the state in a military coup that resulted in hundreds of deaths.

CIVIL-MILITARY GOVERNMENT, 1963-1971

The military's growing autonomy and sense of institutional identity was to be melded with the conservative PNH. Colonel López Arellano joined with a crafty and experienced Nationalist politician, Ricardo Zúñiga Augustinius, to prepare for Constituent Assembly elections in 1965. With the Liberals in disarray and the National party firmly in control of the electoral machinery, the vote results were destined to assure López Arellano his place as chief of state from 1965 to 1971. Promoted to general and elected president, López appointed Zúñiga A. as his secretary of the presidency. The general and his National party collaborator gathered the reins of power through patronage and cautious delegation of authority. Centralized control lent a highly partisan flavor to the administration, but it also provided a focal point for those who grew restless with the government's failure to stimulate a slowed-down economy.

Once past the electoral and constitutional formalities of 1965, López Arellano was to face another set of crises. Structural change was still underway and had helped to spawn new social and economic strata in Honduras; a war with neighboring El Salvador jolted the nation and its armed forces; the obsolescence of traditional caudillo politics was to become much more evident.

The conservative, antireformist nature of the López government surfaced in 1968. Coercion and other illegal tactics were used in municipal elections, after which the National party controlled almost 90 percent of the local governments. Later in the year, the National Congress ratified the Protocol of San José—a Central American Common Market (CACM) agreement designed to limit non-CACM imports. Under the terms of the protocol, consumer taxes were levied in August, precipitating calls for a general strike.[5] The strike was restricted primarily to the northern departments of Yoro, Atlántida, and Cortés with only mild support from Tegucigalpa. A thirty-day state of seige was declared. The government shut down or controlled the mass media and arrested some business and many labor leaders. One week after the Union of the Tela Railroad Company Workers (SITRATERCO) and the Labor Federation of National Workers (FESITRANH) had unadvisedly entered into the strike, they were forced to call it off. With public opinion undercut and the North Coast business community wavering, the labor movement found itself isolated.

The highly authoritarian behavior of the López Arellano government and its seeming disregard for bureaucratic corruption aroused the ire of several North Coast business and labor organizations. These groups had been holding informal meetings to explore mutual concerns over the economic decline and the failure of governmental action on the 1965-1969 National Development Plan. In a communication to President López Arellano, leaders of the Cortés Chamber of Commerce (CCIC) and the FESITRANH expressed their dismay and frustration.

This collaboration between private sector and labor organizations was new for Honduras and was to have a significant impact upon the constellation of political forces over the next decade. Both López Arellano and Zúñiga A. reacted to the nascent challenge. Zúñiga A. feared disruption of National party control if other sectors were effectively brought into the policymaking process. The president began to sense difficulties with his intentions of continuing in power beyond 1971.

Much earlier, in April and May of 1968, the North Coast labor and business leaders had met with the president, cabinet members, and military commanders to discuss the government's indecisive policy. With growing impatience, the group pressed for the involvement of all socioeconomic sectors in the policymaking process and demanded some action designed to break the inertia and corruption within the public bureaucracy. The following year, as land invasions became more frequent in rural areas, the labor movement reiterated demands for effective economic and social reforms. In a historical document, the Confederation of Honduran Workers (CTH) discussed the failure of popular-sector integration into national life. Political instability was attributed to excessive sectarianism on the part of both Liberal and National parties, and the CTH called for a national dialogue that would promote understanding between public and civil sectors.[6] But any immediate response that the document might have drawn was diverted by the conflict with El Salvador in July 1969.

The fast-breaking war brought two thousand deaths, created refugees in both countries, and left a simmering breach in Central American relations until 1980 (see Chapter 6). The conflict seriously depleted the resources and health of the Honduran economy, making worse those conditions that were decried prior to the outbreak of hostilities. But the conflict also dramatically changed Honduran political perspectives and the constellation of political forces. A national unity had been forged in support of the willing, but shorthanded, Honduran armed forces. Despite the repression suffered by the rural peasantry under the López-Zúñiga government, it was the peasants who sacrificed time and energy during the height of the growing season (when their resources were at a minimum) to retrieve the wounded and to feed troops from their own scarce provisions.

The national crisis allowed all social sectors to play a role in defense of the country. The public's reaction to the Salvadoran invasion demonstrated the ability and desire of Honduras to participate collectively in the country's affairs. The war and its aftermath played an important part in changing perspectives of certain factions within the armed forces. For one, repressive tendencies were moderated as younger military officers, influenced by the Peruvian model of reform, appreciated the opportunity to seek a more positive image as "defender of the nation."

The El Salvador–Honduras conflict also provided the opportunity for Honduras to pull out of CACM. Withdrawal from the economic pact had been considered before 1969 because of pressures on the country's balance of trade within CACM. The separation brought at least a short-term benefit for the newer industrial and commercial elites of Honduras, who were then able to supply the domestic market unhindered by competition from Guatemalan, Costa Rican, and Salvadoran industrial products.

Soon after the 1969 war, Hondurans had to cope with the devastating effects of a hurricane that hit the North Coast. The problems of national development were aggravated further, and the dialogue over economic development and national integration was resumed with special urgency. The CTH, the Honduran Council of Private Enterprise (COHEP), and the CCIC revived the issues contained in the now familiar CTH document presented to the public earlier in the year. In November 1969, a momentous conference—to which business leaders, government officials, and representatives from labor and peasant organizations were invited—served as a forum where the various sectors could discuss national development and the apparent political impasse. This "Fuerzas Vivas" conference served to notify the political parties, the government, and the military that certain elements of the business sector, labor organizations, and the peasant movement were no longer quiescent. Issues of presidential succession and the forthcoming elections were being confronted early.

The following year, labor and North Coast business leaders presented an outline of a future national unity plan to President López Arellano.[7] Between February and December 1970, several developments had accelerated a convergence toward some type of political agreement between interest groups and the traditional political parties. Excepting the president himself and perhaps some groups within the military, no political or socioeconomic sector looked favorably upon López Arellano's continuance in office. The National party and Ricardo Zúñiga also had designs upon the presidency. Furthermore, if free elections were held, the Liberal party sensed that victory could be theirs in 1971. To this end, the Liberals supported the position of no reelection.

After serious discussions in a December meeting from which Ricardo Zúñiga was excluded, President López Arellano agreed to support a proposal to the political parties (Planteamiento a los Partidos), not only as chief of state but also in his capacity as head of the armed forces. The proposal recommended a single candidate for president to be selected by both parties. The new chief executive would then choose a cabinet based upon expertise, drawing candidates from all political and social sectors in accordance with Article 4 of the constitution.[8] Both parties would be represented equally in the National Congress. The second portion of the document was a Minimal Plan of Government, which outlined the goals and objectives of the next administration.

Formal and informal consultations among the parties, government, and group representatives lasted throughout December into January 1971. On January 7, the president, giving his support as head of the armed forces, formally announced the Political Plan for National Unity, or Pacto, as it came to be called. It was signed by the political parties, although reluctantly so, and the "guarantors" of the agreement. The major difference from the original proposal was that free elections would decide among rival candidates which party would gain the presidency.[9]

Criticism directed at the agreement contended that it was an alliance of the traditional power elites. In effect, it was merely a mutual defense agreement that would enable the status quo to be maintained in the face of challenges to the traditional system of political power and control. The political parties, faced with an offer they could not refuse, had drawn together to protect their weakened flanks in the changing political system.

THE PACTO GOVERNMENT, 1971–1972

For the March elections, Jorgé Bueso Arias and Ramón Ernesto Cruz were chosen respectively as the Liberal and National party presidential candidates. A National party victory, reversing expectations, placed Ramón Cruz in office and gave the Nationalists control of Congress by one vote. Ricardo Zúñiga became minister of government and justice, assuming a critical role in filling government positions and placing the Nationalist politician at a central point for the disbursement of public funds.

It was soon evident that national unity under the Pacto had become National party domination, with the minister of government functioning as a de facto chief of state. President Cruz was unable or unwilling to act decisively amid heavy criticism of his "do-nothing" government. In February 1972, crisis erupted when peasants and the Special Security Forces (CES) clashed at Talanquera in the department of Olancho. Six farmers and one police sergeant were killed. Labor and peasant movements briefly united in opposition to the regime, but opposition crystallized more when President Cruz dismissed the minister of labor, Gautama Fonseca, and another cabinet officer without consulting the Liberal party.

Cracks in the facade of shared political power were now visible. Overly manipulated by his minister of government, President Cruz was being politically bypassed. The CTH labor organization and the disoriented Liberal party joined and called upon the "guarantors" to review the sixteen-month-old agreement between the parties. Meetings held at the "Francisco Morazán" Military School, mediated by General López Arellano, failed to resolve any of the central issues.

A few weeks before the Pacto review sessions, at a semiclosed meeting in Tela, the Pacto guarantors conferred with each other just before General López Arellano spoke at a massive May Day rally of over twenty-five thousand people. After wide-ranging discussions, a consensus emerged that stronger measures would have to be taken if neither the parties nor President Cruz would comply with the goals stipulated in the National Unity agreement (Pacto). In his speech, López Arellano referred to the economic stagnation and the critical social crises in Honduras. He noted that "the unionized workers of our country are the forgers and creators of our collective wealth; unions have become the school of experience. . . . The Armed Forces are composed of workers and peasants . . . , the Armed Forces are not enemies of the workers and the peasant."[10]

With the collapse of the Pacto review talks, political tensions rose once more. The National Association of Honduran Peasants (ANACH) was prepared to back up its demands for effective agrarian reform with a "hunger march" on the capital city. The biggest labor organizations favored the march and offered logistical support. On the morning of December 4, 1972, President Cruz was sent home by the military, which then formally installed Gen. Oswaldo López Arellano as chief of state.

The coup was received calmly by most citizens, even with relief, as uncertainty about the political future lessened with the return of the general. López Arellano, whose early successes were in part linked to those of the National party, at some point had reconsidered his relationship to the party and its leader, Ricardo Zúñiga. The Salvadoran conflict, the drastic state of the economy, and the more frequent and intense demands of progressive and popular-sector interest groups reinforced a growing awareness within the armed forces that the traditional political institutions were failing. The elites of the National and Liberal parties had never responded adequately to rapidly evolving pressures for modernization. The political parties had had little alternative but to react positively to the Pacto idea, yet they had failed to measure up to the task that was placed before them.

4

The Era of Military Rule, 1972–1982

The early December 1972 coup finally established the Honduran military as governors, this time for nearly ten years. The decade of military rule was influenced by a mixture of personalism, concern for national development, significant reforms, and the dynamics of shifting political coalitions. The initial impetus of reform lost momentum after 1975. The period ended on a note of anxiety and hope as the Nicaraguan revolution unfolded, and national elections led Hondurans back toward constitutional government.

REFORMIST PERIOD, 1972–1975

The direct military intervention was the third in sixteen years, and in each case, Gen. Oswaldo López Arellano had been involved. On this occasion, the internal weakness of the National Unity (Pacto) government along with public disenchantment made it easy for the armed forces to assume control. In effect, the military filled what increasingly had become a political vacuum.[1] The traditional political parties were disregarded as López Arellano and his cabinet of reformist-minded "technocrats" sought to implement progressive social and economic policies. The National Congress was disbanded; and it was declared that the military would remain in power for at least the next five years.

The third administration of López Arellano was distinct because its civilian power base was an informal alliance, or entente, among the armed forces, the CTH and its peasant affiliate, the ANACH, and the progressive private-sector coalition that had been forged gradually after 1968. Many high-ranking officers were influenced by reformist concepts as they related to national development and security. In the context of spreading unrest and the more confident posture of organized labor, the 1972–1975 phase of military rule evolved into a so-called populist government emphasizing economic and social reforms.

Agrarian reform, long demanded by the active peasant movement, was seen as critical to any long-term resolution of Honduran development problems. Moreover, a political debt was owed ANACH for its role in the December coup. Three weeks after assuming office, Decree Law No. 8 was issued, providing for the forced rental, or transfer, of idle or "inadequately utilized" private lands for a period of up to two years. At the same time, leaders of the National Federation of Agriculturalists and Stockraisers of Honduras (FENAGH) were demanding revisions of the law. Their concerns focused on specific clarifications and how the law was to be implemented. After persistent requests, FENAGH leaders and López Arellano met, after which adjustments were made in the administration of Decree Law No. 8. The large landholders had won a concession without having to concede much in return.[2] On the other side of the issue, the major peasant organizations, though still supportive of the government, were less than ecstatic. Decree Law No. 8 was regarded as partial, temporary, and unlikely to transform the basically inequitable structure of land tenancy in Honduras.

Other measures were taken to consolidate the administration's support among labor and some business sectors. The collection of union dues from nonmembers was authorized where such individuals enjoyed the same benefits under collective bargaining contracts. The Institute for Professional Development (INFOP) was established to teach vocational and technical skills. In June 1973, Decree Law No. 49 extended credits and tax exemptions originally granted to individuals and businesses under the 1958 development law.

In January 1974, the chief of state announced a fifteen-year National Development Plan that would enhance national goals and promote domestic social and economic reforms. Two weeks later, the Honduran Forestry Development Corporation (COHDEFOR) was created to administer those aspects of the plan related to forest industries. Nearly 15 percent of the country's export income came from wood products, but the industry was highly concentrated with many enterprises owned by foreigners. COHDEFOR would provide for direct access to tax revenues and help to regain national control over an important resource.

A new Agrarian Reform Law (Decree No. 170) was promulgated on 1 January 1975. As foreseen by landholders, the properties that had been transferred under Decree Law No. 8 were declared expropriated and assigned to the current peasant farmers. There were provisions for the establishment of collectively owned enterprises that would bring together an average of one hundred families for each operation. The law, with its 180 articles, also included a prodigious amount of legal procedures, definitions, and restrictions. Although this was the third major law to deal with agrarian reform, it was not intended seriously to affect the general pattern of landownership. Furthermore, regulations governing the implementation of the new Agrarian Reform Law were delayed and were not published until late 1975.

For General López Arellano and Honduras, 1975 was a turbulent year fraught with collisions between impatient reformists and angry, fearful conservatives. The confrontations took place in rural Honduras, within the ranks of the military, and among the still very active and expanding interest groups, new political movements, and historical political parties. The year included a change in the chief executive, a scandal involving high government officials and the multinational corporation of United Brands, new state policies on banana production and marketing, and a reorganization of the armed forces that further immersed the military governors into policymaking roles.

The reformist stance of the first military administration engendered widespread resistance both domestically and regionally, as Anastasio Somoza grumbled about "communist" land reform in Honduras. Conservative factions in the military were beginning to chafe, while civilian conservatives were finally regrouping. The business community had resolved some of its internal disputes since the disastrous National Unity (Pacto) government had collapsed. Discussions within both Liberal and National parties explored various strategies to combat the "leftward" drift of the military governors and to devise some means of returning to constitutional rule.

Criticisms over the problems and pace of recovery after a 1974 hurricane and discontent over reformist policies encouraged junior military officers to assume more active policy roles. Whether from impatience or concern about the integrity of the armed forces, critics flourished within the military's officer corps. In March 1975, the Movement of Junior Officers, some of whom were battalion commanders, forced the retirement of forty senior officers. That same month the command structure of the military had been reorganized into the Superior Council of the Armed Forces (CONSUFFAA—also referred to as the Superior Council). And it was under CONSUFFAA's decree that the retirement orders had been issued. A few days later, General López Arellano returned from a medical visit to Miami to find himself replaced as head of the armed forces by Col. Juan Alberto Melgar Castro. The chief of state had held the military post since the late 1950s. The new appointment, backed by CONSUFFAA, was the first concrete sign of erosion in the general's political control over the armed forces.

The turning point for López Arellano came a few days later when an article in the *Wall Street Journal* alleged that high government officials had been paid a $1.25 million bribe by United Brands in return for a reduction in the tax on banana exports.[3] The original tax proposal had been one dollar per forty-pound box. The actual tax, when finally levied, was only twenty-five cents, saving United Brands an estimated $75 million per year in export fees. Implicated in the whole sordid affair were the chief of state himself and his economic minister, Abraham Bennatón Ramos. The general formed a "blue-ribbon" investigating commission, but denied it permission to legally examine his personal financial records. It was this refusal that provided an opportunity for CONSUFFAA to replace López Arellano as chief of state on 22 April 1975.

CONSERVATIVE RESURGENCE, 1975–1980

General Oswaldo López Arellano had been centrally involved in Honduran politics for some nineteen years, a period comparable to that of the infamous national caudillo Carías. Though not a caudillo in the classic sense, López Arellano understood and utilized the forms of caudillo politics in creating and manipulating political support among his civilian counterparts. The second phase of military rule was marked by a shift in the institutional growth of the Honduran military. The personalism of López Arellano was gradually outflanked by a broadened, collegial style of authority. CONSUFFAA, composed of twenty-five to thirty battalion, zone, and staff commanders, appointed Col. Juan Alberto Melgar Castro as chief of state, but installed Col. Policarpo Paz García as head of the armed forces. The effect was to broaden authority, with ultimate power residing within the Superior Council.

The forty-five-year-old Melgar Castro, associated with National party politicians, was sympathetically received by Honduran conservatives, who now expected a more receptive ear for their concerns. Yet a CONSUFFAA spokesman indicated that the military governors would not return the government to irresponsible political elites who had neglected the needs of the poor and illiterate masses. He also stated that the colonels would stay in office as long as necessary, whether five or ten years.[4] This seeming contradiction was to be reflected in the apparent indecisiveness of the Melgar Castro period of military rule. Policy wavered between continuing the momentum of the López Arellano "reforms" and appeasing the conservative biases of the Honduran civilian and military political elites.

Agrarian unrest festered as the Superior Council had yet to define its policy toward the enduring agrarian issue. The first test came in May and June 1975 when ten thousand peasants from the National Peasant Union (UNC) occupied over one hundred haciendas. Harassed by members of the stock raisers' association and threatened with forceful action by the army, most peasants withdrew as negotiations were resumed with the National Agrarian Institute (INA).

Land invasions and occupations continued as officials tried to sidestep any direct response to peasant demands. The climate of growing tension was interrupted by tragedy on 25 June 1975 when local ranchers, with assistance from local military officers, invaded a peasant training center near Juticalpa in the department of Olancho. Three weeks later, the decomposed, mutilated bodies of six who had been "arrested" were found in a water well located on property of a rancher who had been involved in the assault. A special military commission investigated and charged four military officers and two ranchers with the killings. The commission also castigated the FENAGH for conducting a campaign of hate and fear against peasants and INA. As rural conditions deteriorated, the major peasant groups put aside some of their differences to form a United Peasant Front.[5] The front released an October ultimatum demanding that the long-delayed but continuously promised land distribution finally commence. Little happened, but during the first week of November, fifteen peasants who had occupied uncultivated but private land in the department of Lempira were killed by paid gunmen.

Symbolic steps were taken, but the military governors were hesitant about pushing ahead vigorously on any large-scale land-distribution program comparable to that achieved under Decree Law No. 8. Active resistance from large landowners, the important multinationals, and sympathetic army officers kept Melgar Castro and CONSUFFAA off balance. A firm, clarified position of agrarian reform never fully developed as INA directors continued to operate without much power within the administration.

The political fallout over the Honduran "bananagate" had facilitated a change in military leaders. It also coalesced the energies of the Honduran political system in a review of the banana-export industry and its impact upon the nation's economy. Pressure from peasant organizations prompted Melgar Castro to take action. The decision to expropriate 23,000 hectares belonging to the Standard Fruit Company was a historical departure, although perhaps not as bold as it could have been. In the wake of hurricane Fifi in 1974, Standard had suggested that the Honduran government help restore the company plantation at Isletas in the department of Colón. This proposal was rejected, and Standard Fruit laid off or fired seven hundred workers. The outraged Unified Sindicate of Standard Fruit Company Workers (SUTRASFCO) demanded that the company be nationalized. The expropriation followed, and a cooperative enterprise composed of the former banana workers was formed under the aegis of the 1975 Agrarian Reform Law to own and work the lands now abandoned by Standard Fruit. Surprisingly, the Isletas cooperative earned a $200,000 profit from its first sales.

Other steps taken in 1975 (to be covered in detail in Chapter 7), included establishment of an Advisory Commission for National Banana Policy, control of North Coast docks by the National Port Enterprise (ENP), acquisition of rail lines from the fruit companies, authorization of the Honduran Banana Corporation (COHBANA), participation in the Union of Banana Exporting Countries (UPEB), and expropriation of more lands by INA. These measures indicated that reformist factions within CONSUFFAA were still able to respond to demands made by labor and peasant movements. However, the discontent of the conservative forces was intense and vituperative. Melgar Castro, either because of his personal inclination, an insecure power base, or both, wavered throughout his administration between extending reforms initiated under

López Arellano or retreating from them in the face of conservative criticism. In January 1977, Enrique Flores Valeriano, the sympathetic Labor minister, was removed from his post. A host of junior officers were given new assignments or sent abroad to fill various diplomatic missions. Lt. Col. Mario Maldonado Muñoz, originally appointed by López Arellano as director of the National Agrarian Institute, was dismissed and sent to Washington, D.C. These actions helped to disperse the reformist elements in the military. And they marked a turning away from "populist" tendencies and the resurgence of more conservative policies and traditional political elites.

Confusing this trend, and perhaps reinforcing the apparent indecisiveness of General Melgar Castro, was the organization of a Presidential Advisory Council (CONASE) in early 1976. The most specific task of the council was to devise a new electoral law in preparation for Constituent Assembly elections scheduled for 1979. CONASE included forty-eight members from all organized sectors, the government, and members of the armed forces. But the advisory council was hampered from the start by several legal and political obstacles. It did not have the authority to pass legislation. It was, in turn, influenced by CONSUFFAA; any advice offered by CONASE could be ignored by government leaders. Labor, peasants, leftists, and other political movements welcomed the slight political opening, but the historical political parties and their allies rejected CONASE and refused to participate in its sessions. The Liberal and National political parties agreed that elections were desirable, but indicated that the presidential advisory council was a needless exercise and expense to the state.

CONASE eventually did produce an electoral law that was approved by CONSUFFAA after some adjustments. Electoral boards would regulate registration and voting procedures for elections originally scheduled for mid-1979, but later postponed until 1980.

Melgar Castro's personal ambitions surfaced as the head of state undertook a subtle campaign that might end with the general as a formally elected president. The delay in the electoral process and encouragement given to newer political movements further alienated Honduran conservatives. It apparently also raised some eyebrows within the ranks of the armed forces. By mid-1978, disputes within the military officer corps over cabinet appointments and replacements were aggravated by a series of newspaper articles that placed the integrity of the armed forces in a bad light. Allegations were made that suggested military complicity in past peasant massacres, collusion with the banana companies, and involvement with illicit drug traffic. Factionalization within CONSUFFAA and the general's reluctance to challenge the allegations against the military institution led to another unscheduled change in government. CONSUFFAA announced the resignation of General Melgar Castro as chief of state and the installation of a new governing triumvirate led by Gen. Policarpo Paz García, head of the armed forces.

With most of its support from landowners, stock raisers, and the National party—led by the ever-present opportunist, Ricardo Zúñiga—the third phase of military rule constituted an end to popular-sector reforms. Though affirming support for the scheduled elections, the junta dissolved CONASE. The period was characterized by more conservative economic and social policies, a concern for social peace and political order, and consolidation of control over the state apparatus. Infrastructure development was emphasized over social-impact programs, more attention was paid to maintaining public order, and administrative control was tightened through Regional Development Councils (Juntas Regionales de Desarrollo).

The military governors emphasized national development policy via expansion of the role of state agencies and increased levels of public-sector investment. Since 1972, a multitude of semiautonomous and autonomous state entities had been created to organize and assist in the development of certain economic sectors such as forestry, banana production, and small-business investment. The Regional Development Councils were set up to coordinate state and private investments and program implementation; headed by the regional military commander, in effect the development councils extended the military's control.

REGIONAL CRISIS AND ELECTIONS

While the military leaders solidified greater administrative control over the state, domestic events and crises within Central America made it imperative for Honduran leaders to respond to demands for social and economic changes. Unresolved problems at the Texaco refinery in Puerto Cortés continued amidst worker discontent, climbing energy costs, and an apparent division with CONSUFFAA over energy development policy. As the conflict erupted between the Somoza regime and the Sandinistas, tension between forces of change and the old order accelerated in Central America. The Nicaraguan revolution unfolded into 1979 while the Honduran government attempted to maintain a position of neutrality and noninterference in the affairs of its neighbors. In fact, the Nicaraguan affair had a variety of external participants. More important, from the perspective of Tegucigalpa, were the possible ramifications for national security and domestic social peace. At the end of 1980, nearly eight thousand refugees from Nicaragua found themselves in Honduras along with many members of the fallen Somoza's national guard. Conditions in El Salvador worsened, and refugees fleeing that country's violence raised the number of refugees in Honduras. The regional crisis now lent an urgency to the process of resolving the eleven-year-old dispute between El Salvador and Honduras. In November 1980, a peace treaty was signed after years of mediation by the Organization of American States and a Peruvian diplomat.

The events that reverberated through Central America were juxtaposed with the Honduran Constituent Assembly elections. These elections, the first of any kind since 1971, were an important step in the transition from military rule to a resumption of civilian political participation in Honduras. The registration of voters was the responsibility of local and national election boards. All political parties had a representative on the National Election Board (TNE). Nevertheless, there was suspicion that these elections would not be as free or open as declared. The National party (PNH) seemed to have the advantage since it had been able to place many of its members into departmental and local government jobs. Gen. Policarpo Paz García and other military leaders appeared to be more receptive to Nationalist entreaties than to those of the still mistrusted Liberal party (PLH). Conditions leading up to the 20 April 1980 election date looked quite similar to those of 1965, when Gen. Oswaldo López Arellano had become an elected chief of state.

To complaints of voter registration irregularities, there was added another controversy over the legal inscription of the Christian Democratic party (PDCH). After ten years, the Innovation and Unity party (PINU) had had its official status approved by the TNE. But on a transparent legal technicality, the Nationalists were able to block official recognition of the PDCH. The Christian Democrats lost an appeal before the Supreme Court—another institution then dominated by the National party.[6] Convinced the elections were to be manipulated, the Christian Democrats called upon all "progressive democrats" to abstain from participation in the charade and declared that the party was ready to work with other sectors to find a just solution to the Honduran political crisis. The formation of a Honduran Patriotic Front (FPH) in February 1980, gathered together the Christian Democrats with several popular-sector and other civic groups. Many had participated in CONASE from 1976 to 1978, where they had labored over the electoral law itself.

As the 1980 elections neared, the United States was most concerned that Honduras demonstrate that peaceful change was feasible in the now troublesome Central America. Many Hondurans, though hopeful, were still wary that elections would only serve to extend military rule in the guise of General Paz García as president of the republic. A few days before the election date, the military leader issued a proclamation calling on all political parties and citizens to participate in an open and honest electoral process. Neither the general nor any other member of the armed forces harbored any aspirations to be president. The Constitutent Assembly would devise a new constitution, and Hondurans would have the opportunity to elect the next president, a congress, and local officials. Over one million Hondurans went to the polls to select delegates for the assembly. With 81 percent of registered voters turning out, the Liberal party won 49.4 percent of the popular vote, the Nationalists 42.2 percent, and PINU trailed with 3.5 percent (see Table 3.2 and 4.1). The system of proportional representation allowed PINU to gain three seats in the Constituent Assembly. This placed the party in a position to play a potential balancing role in the assembly.[7]

TABLE 4.1
Honduran Electoral Data by Department, 1980

Department	Liberal Party	National Party	Innovation Party	Total Vote[a]	Registered Voters
Atlántida	26,927–54.1%[b]	18,392–36.9%[b]	2,372–4.8%[b]	49,797–77.4%[c]	64,329
Colón	13,121–55.8	8,444–35.9	619–2.6	23,512–72.1	32,617
Comayagua	30,423–50.6	25,684–42.7	1,424–2.4	60,091–82.6	72,766
Copán	29,254–45.2	31,526–48.7	1,366–2.1	64,767–85.7[d]	75,606
Cortés	83,646–59.5	42,571–30.3	7,475–5.3	140,595–76.7[d]	183,372
Choluteca	26,786–41.4	32,527–50.3	2,565–4.0	64,650–81.6	79,211
El Paraíso	33,027–56.4	22,478–38.4	888–1.5	58,594–81.4	71,998
Fr. Morazán	75,232–48.1	65,847–42.1	8,518–5.4	156,508–82.5	189,631
Gracias a Dios	1,890–43.2	2,141–48.9	104–2.4	4,376–67.2	6,519
Intibucá	10,558–33.7	18,420–58.7	594–1.9	31,364–83.8	37,411
Islas Bahía	2,172–45.1	2,393–49.7	147–3.1	4,819–76.2	6,324
La Paz	14,400–49.1	12,773–43.6	586–2.0	29,312–86.9	33,729
Lempira	15,868–33.7	27,165–57.7	1,347–2.9	47,075–80.9	58,218
Ocotepeque	11,443–47.6	11,231–46.7	387–1.6	24,041–85.7	28,070
Olancho	29,059–49.7	25,303–43.3	1,748–3.0	58,453–79.7	73,351
Santa Bárbara	38,514–49.6	34,060–43.8	2,366–3.1	77,683–84.9	91,470
Valle	14,016–45.7	14,866–48.4	505–1.7	30,698–82.5	37,195
Yoro	39,432–54.6	27,821–38.5	2,033–2.8	72,187–78.5	91,939
Republic	495,768–49.4%	423,642–42.2%	35,044–3.5%	1,003,470–81.3%	1,233,756

Source: Tribunal Nacional de Elecciones, "Resultado de las elecciones para diputados a la Asamblea Nacional Constituyente, 20 abril de 1980." Tegucigalpa, D.C., June 1980.

[a]Totals include blank and null ballots.

[b]Percentage of total vote

[c]Percentage of registered voters

[d]Total does not include 4,948 votes for independent candidates.

The Liberal victory reflected a growing antimilitary attitude among voters and a reaction to excessive National party political deception. The peaceful election contrasted sharply with escalating violence in El Salvador and the recent civil war in Nicaragua. This so-called oasis of peace was perhaps more apparent than real, as the traditional political parties reverted to habitual arguments over electoral results and whether the next step should be direct or indirect election of the next president of the republic.[8] The debate continued for two months prior to installation of the assembly in July 1980. The overall scene, reminiscent of former good old days, was disappointing to most citizens and caused no little dismay among members of the armed forces. After eight years of political order and careful construction of national development policy, military leaders wondered whether the traditional civilian elites were prepared or able to administer a state apparatus that had been enlarged and that had become more complicated.

Amid the political maneuvers and the military's caution, the National Constituent Assembly (ANC) named Gen. Policarpo Paz García provisional president of the republic. Only the three Innovation party delegates abstained in an otherwise unanimously approved resolution. Roberto Suazo Córdova, the Liberal party leader, was selected as president of the ANC. The Liberals, however, almost lost the power they had won in the national elections. The Nationalists were able to gain control over several state agencies through appointment of their followers to ministerial posts. And with military officers occupying the posts of defense, foreign affairs, and communications, and other appointments subject to approval by CONSUFFAA, the Liberals were in danger of being outflanked despite winning a solid majority of the popular vote. The electoral victory had been converted into a weak government that the armed forces were able to dominate easily. This fourth phase of military-led government was to last nearly two years.

The ANC settled down to work on the laborious tasks of revising the election law and constructing a new constitution, the country's fourteenth since 1838. Elections for president of the republic, a National Congress, and local municipal officials were set for 29 November 1981. Although they retreated from daily policy implementation, the military governors were able to project their own interests into the process of returning government to civilian hands. The Constituent Assembly attempted to investigate allegations of corruption involving public officials and government agencies. But at a face-to-face meeting, Liberal and National party deputies were flatly told that the 1981 elections would be canceled if they persisted in the proposed investigation. The message was clear—informal, dubious arrangements and income of senior military officers were not to be breached.

Election Campaign

Throughout 1981, most Hondurans were preoccupied with a deteriorating economy and political campaigns leading toward the No-

National party political propaganda for its 1981 presidential candidate—Ricardo
Zúñiga A.

vember elections. The National party promoted its candidate on a
campaign of experience, law and order, and anticommunism. Ricardo
Zúñiga, the PNH leader, stated that Hondurans could expect the same
service and performance he provided during the first government of
López Arellano (1965–1971). The PLH, meanwhile, had to cope with
its customary factionalism. Roberto Suazo Córdova kept the conservative
wing intact by excluding the Popular Liberal Alliance (ALIPO) from
participation in the PLH primary elections.[9]

Meanwhile, the PDCH had been granted legal recognition and the
right to participate in the forthcoming national elections. It spread a
radical message of social transformation and hoped to galvanize a
significant though small percentage of the electorate behind the party
candidate, Dr. Hernán Corrales Padilla. The Pinuistas and their leader,
Dr. Miguel Andonie Fernández, advocated principles of honest, efficient
government and basic reforms and called for a national dialogue to air
the country's social and economic problems.

The militant left, including the various Marxist-Leninist political
movements, decided to participate via the FPH. The elections were
viewed as an opportunity to present an alternative message to the
Honduran people. Nominating independent candidates in three departments (Copán, Cortés, and Yoro) opened the political process slightly,
even though there was little chance of winning representation in the
National Congress.[10]

Again, the 1981 campaign was disoriented by acrimonious cries of fraud in voter registration and manufactured rumors of a military coup. The PNH now claimed that the Liberal-dominated TNE had discriminated against Nationalist party members in its purge of the polling lists. Some factions within the armed forces probably welcomed any possible chance to cancel the elections, but competition within CONSUFFAA left no unity of purpose. On the other hand, General Paz García, as provisional president, had begun to perceive himself as more a solution to the country's problems than either of the traditional political parties' presidential candidates. Venezuelan and Mexican praise (over the transition to civilian rule) added to the general's doubts about leaving power. The idea of a "preventive" coup was generated in conversations with the excluded Liberal party faction of ALIPO. The concept was also entertained by retired Lt. Col. Mario Maldonado Muñoz, who had gathered like-minded supporters into a Movement of Patriotic Renovation (Maldonado had headed the INA during the reformist government of López Arellano from 1972 to 1975).

The 1981 Elections

On 29 November 1981, the first elections in over twenty-five years intended to directly select a president and a congress were held. Over 1.2 million voters went to the polls, giving the Liberal Party of Honduras a convincing 53 percent majority (see Table 4.2). The National Party of Honduras was crushed as the Liberals won control of the National Congress and 61 percent of the municipal governments. The margin of 150,000 votes signifies that the Liberal party factions—ALIPO and the Liberal Unity Front (FUL)—did not desert the party's ranks. The Innovation party held on to its small core of urban-based, middle-class support. Unexpectedly, the Christian Democrats made a dismal showing in their first election, capturing less than 2 percent of the total vote. The independent candidates of the militant left failed miserably, attracting scarcely 4,000 votes or less than 1 percent of the total.[11]

The PLH victories in 1980 and 1981 reflected the public's disenchantment with military governments and a growing concern over public-sector corruption. The PNH suffered accordingly because of its long association with the military and the image of corruption and political manipulation it had developed ever since the military coup in 1963.

In late January 1982, after the new constitution was promulgated, the Liberal administration of Dr. Roberto Suazo Córdova was inaugurated. The celebrations were held in the national soccer stadium, which was filled to capacity by an excited and highly expectant citizenry. High military leaders and foreign dignitaries were in attendance. Although a sour note was contributed by the absence of the newly elected National party congressional delegation and other party leaders, they were all but forgotten as the new president, three vice-presidents designate, members of the Supreme Court, and the new head of the armed forces,

TABLE 4.2
Honduran Electoral Data by Department, 1981

Department	Liberal Party (PLH)	National Party (PNH)	Innovation Party (PINU)	Christian Democrats (PDCH)	Total Vote[a]	Mayoralties PLH	PNH
Atlántida	33,900-56.0%[b]	21,879-36.2%[b]	2,031-3.4%[b]	701-1.2%[b]	60,498	7	0
Colón	17,238-58.0	10,548-35.5	519-1.8	396-1.3	29,719	9	0
Comayagua	36,513-51.7	30,265-42.8	1,180-1.7	962-1.4	70,633	13	6
Copán	33,742-46.2	34,652-47.4	720-1.0	1,104-1.5	73,044[c]	11	12
Cortés	103,720-61.8	47,230-28.2	6,257-3.7	2,286-1.4	167,722[c]	10	1
Choluteca	41,387-46.4	40,667-45.6	2,237-2.5	2,342-2.6	89,242	9	7
El Paraíso	42,276-58.6	26,345-36.5	1,004-1.4	743-1.0	72,164	15	3
Fr. Morazán	109,337-53.5	79,319-38.8	7,134-3.5	2,708-1.3	204,498	23	4
Gracias a Dios	2,687-43.9	3,051-49.8	67-1.1	98-1.6	6,122	1	1
Intibucá	13,878-37.3	21,019-56.5	569-1.5	720-1.9	37,183	3	13
Islas Bahía	2,904-52.4	2,491-44.9	58-1.0	40-0.7	5,545	2	2
La Paz	17,879-51.9	14,774-42.9	418-1.2	327-1.0	34,419	13	6
Lempira	19,923-36.3	31,524-57.4	1,075-2.0	767-1.4	54,902	1	26
Ocotepeque	13,216-49.1	11,708-43.5	396-1.5	943-3.5	26,904	10	6
Olancho	34,013-50.2	28,848-42.6	1,759-2.6	1,416-2.1	67,733	14	8
Santa Bárbara	44,738-49.9	39,500-44.0	1,602-1.8	1,796-2.0	89,672	16	10
Valle	17,755-48.3	16,330-44.5	789-2.1	862-2.3	36,735	7	2
Yoro	51,286-58.2	30,939-35.2	1,604-1.8	952-1.1	88,000[c]	9	2
Republic	636,392-52.4%	491,089-40.4%	29,419-2.4%	19,163-1.6%	1,214,735[d]	173	109

Source: Tribunal Nacional de Elecciones, Tegucigalpa, D.C. (January 1982).

[a]Totals include blank and null ballots.

[b]Percentage of total vote

[c]Totals include independent votes (Copán- 514; Cortés- 2,572; and Yoro- 911).

[d]Total registered voters given as 1,504,658; total vote equals 80.7% turnout.

Street scene in La Paz—hometown of President Roberto Suazo Córdova.

Col. Gustavo Alvarez Martínez, took their oaths of office. In his inaugural speech, President Suazo Córdova stressed that his administration would be a government of "revolution, work, and honesty." Moreover, all national sectors should participate in the policies of austerity and creativity. Only through participatory democracy would national integration be accomplished. The president reminded his countrymen of the regional crisis, alluded to the impending dangers for Honduras and called upon the world to recognize Central America as a zone of peace.[12]

The immediate task of the Suazo Córdova government was to shore up the nation's economy and prevent further erosion of the country's progress in national development. The administration faced difficult decisions—decisions that would dictate policies bound to conflict with rising popular expectations. Economic growth for 1980 and 1981 had slowed drastically, investment levels had declined, and capital flight had accelerated, mainly in response to the spread of violence in El Salvador and tensions emanating from Nicaragua. The national treasury contained a deficit of nearly $100 million, with no immediate prospects of domestic or international financing. The nation's external debt had ascended to almost $1 billion, in part because some decentralized public agencies were unable to maintain debt payments.

Honduras was at a turning point in its political evolution. One direction was toward broader participation in the polity and society in a quest for national integration. The other direction was toward perpetuation of the exclusionary and authoritarian modes of caudillo politics and variations of military rule.

For more than a decade, the Honduran military had wielded power in direct terms. Domestic and international pressures had been exerted since mid-1976 for a return to constitutional government. Under heavy pressure from the United States, the colonels were forced to open the political system. Although the armed forces retreated from power, controls over military affairs were not relinquished, and limitations were placed upon the scope of civilian policy innovation. Given the economic difficulties and intractable administration problems, there remained some expectation of resuming direct power with the "failure" of the Liberal government.

5

The State and Elections

Honduras has had four different constitutions since 1950. The constitution of 1936 continued in force until the Liberal victory in 1957, when the country's twelfth basic law since 1838 was approved by a Constituent Assembly. The thirteenth was promulgated on 3 June 1965, when General López Arellano became president.

The lengthy 1982 constitution was a product of the National Constituent Assembly (ANC), which deliberated from 20 July 1980 to 20 January 1982, just seven days before the Liberal government of Roberto Suazo Córdova assumed office. The document represents little fundamental change in the structure and pattern of Honduran government. The terms of office for president of the republic and congressional deputies were shortened from six to four years. At the same time, the tenure of the head of the armed forces, formally chosen by the National Congress, was changed to five years. This juxtaposition of terms strengthened political dominance of the military by insulating the process of choosing the military commander from the confusion of political campaigns and national elections.

Despite numerous constitutions and often tedious attention to legalities and formalities, the reality of political power in Honduras has been concentration of authority in the hands of the chief of state. Under military rule, while the National Congress was disbanded, the powers of state were further concentrated within the executive branch.

The return of constitutional government in 1982 effected some redistribution of power, particularly since the National Congress has undertaken its legislative tasks with deliberation. In addition, the 1981 elections reinstated popular choice to municipal government—reestablishing an important dimension of citizen participation and foundation for political system legitimacy. The slight dispersal of formal power does not mean, however, that the polity has become significantly less centralized. For one thing, the military retains its place at the center of power and is unlikely to encourage any serious competitors. For another, the growth of the state and the role it fulfills in economic and social policy have expanded. Citizen demands and the several political sectors, accustomed to centralized authority, have even more reason to be attracted to the state and its resources.

EXECUTIVE STRUCTURE

Although Honduran constitutional theory subscribes to the principle of separation of powers, the executive dominates the legislative and judicial aspects of the polity. And despite the historical foundations for local government, any practical autonomy at the local level has been erased by the forces of centralization: monopoly over public funds, technical expertise, and direct political intervention. This is not to say that the authority of the central government has always been extended effectively to all levels and localities, but rather that the measured capacity of Honduran local government has declined over time and has come to depend more upon central funding and direction than upon local resources and decisions.

The original expansion and growth of the Honduran state occurred after 1876 during the era of Liberal reforms. This was also a period when officials encouraged foreign investment and initiated wider international economic contacts. Weak communications, the power of regionally based political caudillos, and the absence of any national political organization inhibited the extension of administrative control throughout Honduras. The historically important Liberal and National political parties did not emerge until after the turn of the century. The void was filled by the personalized authority of political power brokers and the growing presence of foreign-owned mining and agricultural interests.

Progress toward national political consolidation was made during the 1920s and 1930s. Revenues had increased with Honduras's rise to prominence as a leading world producer of bananas, a crop that accounted for up to 80 percent of the nation's export earnings. Both the Liberal and National parties benefited from the web of economic and political ties that had evolved over the years with the United Fruit and Standard Fruit companies. Funds enabled political leaders to strengthen party organizations and influence the loyalties of regional political bosses. But it was not until after 1932, when Tiburcio Carías Andino finally won the presidency, that state authority was effectively extended throughout most of Honduras. Carías accomplished this through his iron control over the National party. His power within the party was aided by a melding of public and private political and financial interests held by Honduran leaders, foreign-owned companies, and other international investors. Also, Carías consolidated his (and the state's) authority with more ruthless methods, sometimes referred to as "burial, exile, and jail."

By 1950, after sixteen years of governing, Carías had instituted the semblance of a state bureaucracy and successfully implemented basic

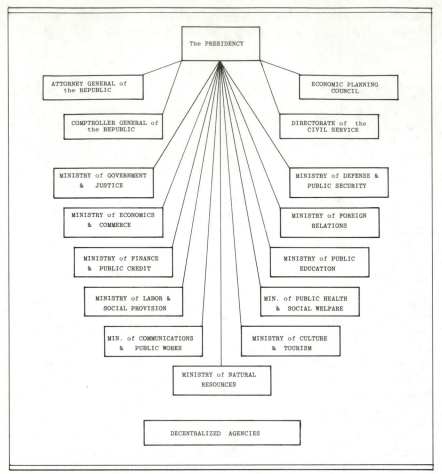

The PRESIDENCY

ATTORNEY GENERAL of
the REPUBLIC

ECONOMIC PLANNING
COUNCIL

COMPTROLLER GENERAL of
the REPUBLIC

DIRECTORATE of the
CIVIL SERVICE

MINISTRY of GOVERNMENT
&   JUSTICE

MINISTRY of DEFENSE &
PUBLIC SECURITY

MINISTRY of ECONOMICS
&   COMMERCE

MINISTRY of FOREIGN
RELATIONS

MINISTRY of FINANCE
&   PUBLIC CREDIT

MINISTRY of PUBLIC
EDUCATION

MINISTRY of LABOR &
SOCIAL PROVISION

MIN. of PUBLIC HEALTH
&   SOCIAL WELFARE

MIN. of COMMUNICATIONS
&   PUBLIC WORKS

MINISTRY of CULTURE
&   TOURISM

MINISTRY of NATURAL
RESOURCES

DECENTRALIZED AGENCIES

Figure 5.1   Organization of the Executive Branch in Honduras, 1981

state services. Although results were still drastically short of Honduran
needs, roads had been constructed, more schools had been built, and
the streets of Tegucigalpa had been paved.

The legacy of personalism and authoritarianism has survived the
vicissitudes of political instability, military rule, and increased demands
for wider political participation. The president of the republic is the
formal and informal center of authority in the Honduran state. This
pattern has been challenged since 1950 by military intervention and
rule. Regardless, the executive-centered nature of the Honduran political
system endures whether the chief of state is an elected civilian politician,
a triumvirate of colonels, or a general of the Honduran armed forces.
The chief executive still appoints (and relieves) all major cabinet officers

(Figure 5.1).[1] He also appoints all eighteen departmental governors representing executive authority with direct influence over local governments. Furthermore, during periods of direct rule (i.e., in lieu of elections) it is the chief executive who ultimately controls the appointment of all local officials. A major exception to this comprehensive power of direct appointment is the selection of the head of the armed forces and members of the Supreme Court. These are the responsibility of the National Congress, although presidential influence is easily extended via political-party loyalties into the legislative branch. But in the absence of the legislature, appointments are made by the chief executive. Also, as the armed forces have emerged over the past three decades, the formal choice of its supreme military leader has rarely been influenced outside military circles.

The pattern of political demands also gravitates toward the presidency. National political interest groups, as well as delegations from villages and hamlets deep in the Honduran wilderness, all seek answers to their problems by direct appeals to the president of the republic. This pattern of authority is derived from the traditional style of personal, individualistic rule, the president as political-party leader, and his symbolic importance as paternal leader. Finally, as the state has grown, the chief executive finds himself at the apex of a government that impacts upon the daily lives of more and more Hondurans. The president in effect is the personification of the new state. Though it may be an administrative agency or a financial institution that actually responds to citizen demands, presidential directives are the historical (cultural) equivalent of the paternalistic caudillo.

The complexity of the executive branch with its evolving technical functions, expanded role in the economy, and multiple social programs has been compounded by the creation of semiautonomous and autonomous state entities such as the National Development Bank, the Honduran Telecommunications Enterprise (HONDUTEL), and the Honduran Institute for Social Security (IHSS). The state apparatus has expanded since 1950 to include more than twenty-seven independent agencies. Between 1970 and 1978, twelve new agencies were authorized. These reflected the state's shift toward higher levels of direct public investment and into commodity production and marketing, infrastructure development, and business subsidies.

The decentralized agencies of the state vary in structure, function, and composition. Agencies are classified as public institutes, public enterprises, or mixed enterprises.[2] *Public institutes* perform those programs or services of a social or collective nature normally not included in private-sector efforts. The Housing Institute (INVA), the National Agrarian Institute (INA), and the Honduran Institute of Anthropology and History (IHAH) are examples of decentralized public agencies.

Public enterprises have their own resource base and, except for the Honduran Forestry Development Corporation (COHDEFOR), are autonomous organisms of the state. COHDEFOR is mandated to manage and protect the renewable resources of Honduras's extensive pine and tropical hardwood forests. The Honduran Banana Corporation (COH-BANA), the National Railroad of Honduras (FNH), the Central Bank of Honduras (BANTRAL), and the National Enterprise of Electrical Energy (ENEE) are other examples of such agencies.

Mixed enterprises are those that bring together both public and private participation. However, in this case, the state retains 51 percent of the capital, and private domestic and foreign investors are limited to a share of 49 percent in any given enterprise. One corporation is the Forest Industry Corporation of Olancho (CORFINO), authorized by Decree Law No. 465 in 1977 to develop and direct the exploitation of the Olancho forest preserve.

This transformation of the executive has paralleled increased budgetary emphases upon what are called categories of the "service state"; that is, functions of social welfare, economic development, and environmental services versus administration, law-and-order functions, and national defense.[3] In the 1978 central government budget and that proposed for 1979, 62 percent was allocated for education, health, natural resources, and development projects such as roads and communications.[4] About one-third of the funding for the Ministry of Natural Resources and the Ministry of Public Health was underwritten by external funding—loans, grants, or other forms of bilateral or multilateral international assistance. Almost 60 percent of the budget of the Ministry of Communications and Public Works came from similar sources. Apart from continued emphasis on education, most public investment policies have been intended to expand the nation's infrastructure.

Another dimension of the state's growth has been the growing number of public employees. Population increases, assumption of new functions by government, and more demands from the public for various services stimulated the formation of new agencies and increased the size of most public bureaucracies. Between 1967 and 1978, the number of central-government employees ranged from twenty-seven thousand to nearly thirty-three thousand. These figures included several thousand teachers in the public school systems. The decentralized agencies provided more public-sector jobs. In 1980, this amounted to just over twenty-two thousand white-collar, clerical, and service personnel. Including teachers, military, and security personnel, there were about seventy-seven thousand employees working for the national government.

Public jobs have been the core of political patronage for the political parties. They are a key method of extending authority and political influence into the rural areas of Honduras. At higher levels, patronage is designed to reward supporters, exercise control over certain policy areas, and co-opt younger political activists. The Nationalists were able to perfect this system during the long period of rule under Carías. With the growth of the state, the traditional parties initially benefited from

Legislative Palace, where the Honduran Congress meets.

the new opportunities to place their supporters into positions of public authority. Under the aegis of military rule, this tendency was moderated somewhat, but the dynamics of "dividing the spoils" still pervades the pre- and postelectoral maneuvers of capturing power.[5]

LEGISLATIVE BRANCH: THE NATIONAL CONGRESS

In contrast to the prominence of executive authority and structure, the legislative function of the National Congress has never fully developed despite elaborate formal principles and powers enumerated in most constitutional documents. This pattern is common to many Latin American polities in that the executive is rarely challenged by legislative authority. Frequently, legislative institutions are merely dissolved and not allowed to function. Both aspects apply to Honduras. The formal legislative body—the National Congress—has rarely functioned as a viable institution.

In formal terms of the 1982 constitution, the unicameral National Congress is directly elected for four-year terms. The number of deputies is allotted among the eighteen departments according to population, with each province guaranteed at least one representative. The body elects its own president and appoints a Permanent Committee that conducts congressional business when the legislature is not in session. In the past, Congress had the task of selecting the president of the republic when electoral results fell short of the required absolute majority. This legality was a key to much of the political confrontation and chaos since 1876. Party delegations occasionally refused to take their seats, thereby preventing a quorum and thwarting the constitutional process. Under the 1982 constitution, Congress declares a president elected when a candidate has won a simple majority of the popular vote, but only when and if the National Election Board fails to do so.

Just as a tradition of legislative debate and independence has not evolved, so too the concept of popular and special-interest representation has failed to develop within the Congress. Candidate selection and the electoral process have been controlled by party organization, resulting in congressional deputies whose socioeconomic interests and political fortunes lay within the province of the traditional political elites. Since 1950, the legislature has functioned only little more than half the time. With this closure of political communication, and given the hierarchical nature of the historical political parties, new socioeconomic sectors and political movements focused their demands directly toward the ministries and other agencies of the executive branch. The political-party channels have been bypassed even when the legislature was in session.

A common trait of Honduran legislative bodies has been the legitimizing function performed by constituent assemblies. Of the seven national elections held between 1950 and 1981 (see Table 3.2), three were for delegates to constituent assemblies. In two cases (1957 and 1965), after drawing up and ratifying new constitutions, these assemblies elected a president of the republic and converted themselves into the National Congress. Thus the selection of both president and congressional deputies was indirect or via "second-order" elections. In the 1980 elections, the majority political faction (Liberals) wavered between the temptation of second-order elections and the risk entailed in new direct elections for president, congress, and local officials. The decision to convert an assembly, rather then being viewed in the light of constitutional or legal principles, can be analyzed in the context of contemporary conditions that surround each assembly.

The issues surrounding the 1980-1981 Constituent Assembly went well beyond the question of which party could control the political process. The military had ceased to be merely the arbiter of political stability and as policymaker had become an integral part of the political process. The armed forces had an institutional interest in national development and the maintenance of social peace. The debate and political maneuvering over whether to proceed with second- or first-order elections were made even more delicate by the environment of the spreading Central American crisis. Any appearance of fraud or political chicanery that might arise from second-order elections could have been "the detonation to explode the charge of accumulated anxieties, mistrust, repressed feelings produced by the long and unjustified de facto situation, military hegemony, and corruption, before which leaders in the traditional political parties would be powerless."[6] Regardless, if the Liberal party had had a solid, guaranteed majority, the tacit approval of military rulers, and the support of the United States, it would have pressed more vigorously to elect a president and convert the assembly into the National Congress.

JUDICIAL GOVERNMENT

The judicial branch of government, ostensibly independent, functions under the influence of party loyalty and executive authority. The Supreme Court of Justice has both original and appellate jurisdiction, receiving cases via writs of cassation and protection (*amparo*). It is able to exercise judicial review in cases involving questions of constitutionality. The court's nine justices are normally elected by the congress for four-year terms. Failing that, they are appointed by the chief executive. Supreme Court justices must be qualified lawyers and have had experience in other courts as magistrates.

The judicial system is administered by the high court with all judges (except justices of the peace) appointed by it. There are eight Appeals Courts, as well as forty Courts of Records that have both original and appellate functions. Arguments in these courts are written, and standards for judges are higher than those for the more than three hundred justice-of-the-peace courts. Justices of the peace occupy the courts of first instance for most law violators. They are appointed by the magistrates who sit on the Courts of Record. In most aspects, the court system has undergone few changes since the early 1900s.

MUNICIPIOS

A centralized system of constitutional and political authority is the picture that has emerged since the advent of Carías and the latter-day growth of the state under the military governors. Despite this trend, local governments remain vitally important to the average citizen for essential services and initial contact with authorities. Local government consists of the 281 *municipios* and the Central District, which combines the twin cities of Tegucigalpa and Comayaguela.[7] These governments were originally formed as corporations exercising powers constitutionally reserved to them. Charged with upholding standards of health, safety, and order, the *municipios* implement public works, collect taxes, and compile vital statistics along with other census data. The municipal level is also where citizens register to vote. Defined as an administrative unit, boundaries are not determined by the extent of urbanized settlement.

Municipal governments normally are elected by local citizens who choose a mayor (*alcalde*), a recorder (*síndico*), and a city council. The councils vary in size according to population but are allowed a maximum of seven councillors. The elected mayor has a double role as administrative head of the *municipio* and, at the same time, the representative of the central government who is charged with carrying out national laws and policies. For the most part, mayors have been forced to fulfill the latter role since most authority and resources have resided with the central government. Other structural changes have accentuated the trend toward centralization as local expenditures decline in relation to overall growth in the gross domestic product. *Municipios* find it difficult to retain or recover much of the collected taxes delivered to the central government, and most are dependent on subsidies that are issued by several ministries in Tegucigalpa. Accentuating this centralization process has been the proliferating character of the state itself. New decentralized agencies such as the INA and the COHDEFOR tend to absorb functions performed by the *municipios,* and in the process they soak up funds and resources formerly available to local governments.

After 1972, mayors and other local officials became more an administrative arm of the central government, since all were appointed by military leaders rather than elected to their posts. Between 1978 and 1980, administrative control by the military governors was tightened when Regional Development Councils were interposed between local and central governments.[8] Each council was headed by the military-zone commander, and the regional representative of the Superior Council of Economic Planning (CONSUPLANE) acted as the technical secretary of the junta. While they functioned, all communications between central and local governments were routed through the regional organisms. The departure from traditional communication channels worked to the benefit of many smaller, poorer *municipios* that usually had been forced to compete with the larger, more urban communities. Trips by mayors and other officials to the capital are expensive and time-consuming propositions. With decision points located at the regional level (i.e., in the guise of military-zone commanders), access to authorities by local governments and response to their requests were facilitated in some cases. Once the 1980-1981 National Constituent Assembly (ANC) was installed (20 July 1980), the Regional Development Councils withered as the military backed away from the day-to-day administrative issues. The ANC asserted itself in matters of overall policy, and the military-zone commanders grew tired of the time-consuming and fatiguing process of political negotiation and bureaucratic competition.

POLITICAL SUCCESSION AND ELECTIONS

The processes of political succession in Honduras have often fit the stereotyped image of men on horseback clashing in armed conflict, with the outcome of these struggles determining who assumed the presidential office. Such conditions promoted political instability and unscheduled changes in government. This was the case during most of the nineteenth century, although there were periods when hotly contested elections were used (or abused) to decide which faction or leader assumed office.

Throughout most of the twentieth century, Honduran political succession has been a mixture of elections, military coups, and *continuismo* (the practice of altering presidential terms and rules of succession through constitutional "adjustments"). Gen. Tiburcio Carías Andino was the first Honduran leader to impose a measure of stability and to consolidate the authority of the state on a national basis. Personal loyalty as a political bond was enhanced as the president and local leaders combined their individual contacts into an effective organization of followers and adherents. For Carías this was the basis of his political machine. The practice of *continuismo* also contributed toward centralization of the polity as Carías, through his National party organization, was able to completely dominate the legislature, the judicial branch, and the actions of local government.

However, the legacy of stability was shortlived once Carías stepped down in 1949. His successor, Juan Manuel Gálvez, carried on until 1954, when national elections were held. But 1954 was also the first time since 1932 that the Liberal party was able to participate openly in the political process. Inconclusive election results marked the beginning of three decades of political confusion and realignment. Between 1954 and 1981, political power shifted irregularly via elections, Constituent Assembly actions, manipulated vote totals, and direct intervention by a modernizing armed forces.

Electoral procedures and results for much of Honduran history generally have not been observed with care or respect. Both of the traditional political parties have utilized corrupt electoral practices, and both have complained of unconscionable fraud and manipulation, each accusing its historical rival. Pejoratively, Hondurans have ridiculed themselves by referring to such elections as Honduran style.

Elections in Honduras have been held every four or six years at the national level, with interim periods for municipal elections. The organization and conduct of elections are entrusted to a National Election Council or Board (TNE).[9] Election boards are also established at the departmental level and in each *municipio*. There are precincts for each three hundred voters. The Supreme Court chooses one member of the National Election Board, and each legally organized party is represented by one member. A similar composition is maintained at lower levels. The TNE, first established under the 1978 election law, is responsible for registering all eligible citizens eighteen years and older. Voting is obligatory, though active military are prohibited from participating in the polling. Women gained equal political rights during the Lozano government and voted in national elections for the first time in 1956. Men and women, however, still report to separate polling places.

In late 1982, the National Congress established the National Register of Persons (Decree Law No. 150) as an adjunct agency to the TNE. The

National Register was to collect all vital statistics—births, deaths, marriages, naturalizations, and so on—tasks usually done by local governments (*municipios*). Once a civil register is established the new agency is charged with issuing national identity cards and compiling a new national electoral census. Delays in implementing the National Register of Persons and widespread dissatisfaction over the 1978-1979 and 1980-1981 voter registration lists caused a postponement of the 1983 municipal elections until a new electoral census could be completed.

For a political party to participate in elections it must be legally inscribed. The Liberal and National political parties, accustomed to each other's challenge, have been reluctant to share political power and have instituted a difficult registration procedure. Parties seeking legal recognition must acquire a series of notarized documents and file a statement of principles, party statutes, and programs. Finally, a party's petition to the TNE must have valid signatures from at least ten thousand registered voters. The process is fraught with difficulties. To register, voters must have the appropriate documents. And the *municipios*, electoral registration procedures, and the election boards have all been controlled by the traditional parties. In some cases, the TNE merely has refused to act; in others, some of the necessary documentation is found to be invalid.

Honduran political structures are faced with continuing pressures for reform and wider participation; yet, for the most part, traditional political elites coalesced within the National and Liberal parties have resisted demands for broader participation. Challenges have appeared from smaller, newer political parties and even within the long-established parties themselves. The question then has become whether the older political elites can successfully adapt to demands for wider citizen participation. Urbanization, economic diversification, proliferating organizations, and rising educational levels all may eventually force a shift in political-party support.

National elections in 1957, 1965, 1971, 1980, and 1981 were conducted under differing political conditions. Interestingly, *all five* were held under the auspices of military governments. In 1957, the elections for a Constituent Assembly were the first that were relatively free and open since 1932 when Carías first came to power. The 1956-1957 military junta fulfilled its stated purpose of providing a climate for honest elections and returning control of the government to the civilian politicians. In an apparent reaction to past National party excesses, and with support of emergent middle sectors, the Liberal party won a majority in every department. The 1965 elections were controlled by General López Arellano and his National party allies. But elections in 1971 were unique since they were conducted under terms of the National Unity agreement (Pacto); it was also the first time in nearly twenty years that Hondurans were able to participate in direct elections for president and members of congress. Overall voter turnout was low (63 percent), partly because of mistrust and cynicism as well as the last minute "deal" between the Liberal and National parties.

From the coup in 1972 until 1980, military rulers gradually assumed more control over the state apparatus. The administrations of López Arellano, Melgar Castro, and Paz García followed one another, and policies grew more conservative. The decade was interspersed with brief but weak attempts to open the political process. Eventually, however, pressures for citizen participation and other demands arising within the political system required some governmental response. The spreading conflict in Central America added a regional dimension to the course of Honduran political change. In Nicaragua and El Salvador the traditional structures of power had failed to adapt or accommodate to the demands that had been building throughout the 1970s. But in 1979 and 1980, the Honduran polity was still flexible enough to respond to such pressures. The military rulers cautiously proceeded with new Constituent Assembly elections scheduled for April 1980 as the first phase of reinstituting constitutional government. With a surprisingly heavy (and peaceful) turnout of over 80 percent of the registered voters, the Liberals upstaged the Nationalists by winning 49.4 percent of the total vote. Under a modified election law, the 1981 elections for president, congressional deputies, and municipal governments were practically a mirror image of the year before. The Liberal party reaffirmed its public mandate to govern for the next four years (1982–1986). However, analysis of voting patterns in the five national elections held between 1957 and 1981 indicates that Liberal party support is closely associated with the more developed and urban regions of Honduras (Figure 5.2).[10] In the central zone of the country (the so-called corridor of development), the Liberal party has won four or five of the elections in all but the departments of Comayagua and Choluteca. Choluteca has customarily been a Nationalist stronghold with effective political control exercised by large landholders and stock raisers. The National party, in general, maintains a solid hold on the more rural and isolated regions, especially those departments that lie along the border with El Salvador. These patterns of urban-rural party support were maintained in the 1981 national elections even as the Liberal party extended its electoral influence into the Nationalist bailiwicks of Copán, Choluteca, and Valle.

It appears that urbanization and socioeconomic development would favor an expanding base of support for the Liberal party. But other factors can affect the preservation of Liberal political support: Factionalization has been a perennial problem for the PLH, and relations between the military and the Liberal party never have been warm or characterized by confidence. Political survival will depend a great deal upon how the armed forces perceive the intentions, capabilities, and performance of party leaders.

The 1980 and 1981 elections demonstrated the willingness of Hondurans to participate in constitutional political processes. They also

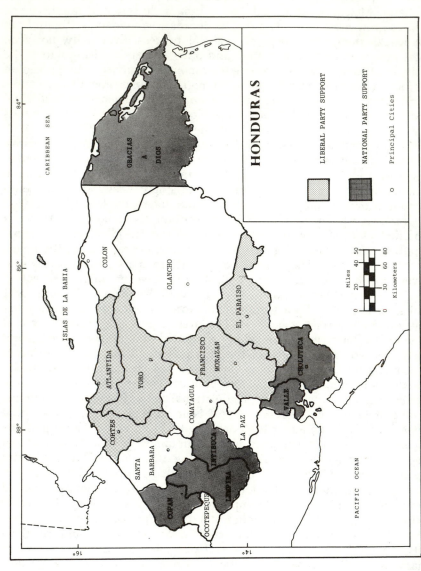

Figure 5.2 Map of Political Support in Honduras by Party and Department

indicated a desire, and pride, on the part of Honduras to avoid the calamity of violence befalling its Central American neighbors. It remains to be seen whether questions of political stability and succession have been resolved. True, roving bands of men led by regional political chiefs (*jefes* or *caciques*) no longer pose a threat to sitting presidents. The traditional caudillo is now personified by generals and colonels who are part of an established military institution. The armed forces of Honduras have become a third major "political party." The military interventions into Honduran politics (1956, 1963, 1972) differ from the nineteenth- and early twentieth-century style, but the pattern of irregular political succession has not changed appreciably. For President Suazo Córdova or another leader to be elected and take office in 1986 would be a historical turning point. It would be the first time since 1932— more than half a century—that a president would take office under regular constitutional procedures.

A woman wearing a souvenir of a Liberal Party political campaign.

A sample of major Honduran newspapers.

(Left) The presidential house. *(Right)* Statue of Honduran writer, politician, and philosopher José Cecilio del Valle in Tegucigalpa.

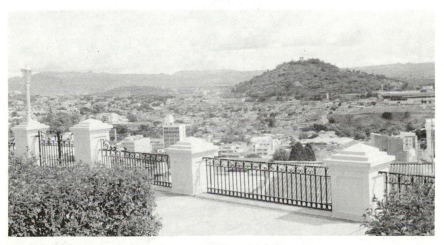

Parque Leona overlooking downtown Tegucigalpa.

The church at Valle de Angeles.

The Municipal Market of Santa
Rosa de Copán.

A small-town general store.

Mt. Picacho is a backdrop for central Tegucigalpa.

6

The Political Sectors

Until the retirement of longtime caudillo Carías in 1949, most individuals participated in the Honduran political system via personal ties to the state and foreign-owned businesses coalesced around the Liberal and National party organizations. Elections were seldom respected; the governing style was paternalistic and authoritarian. Other than the historical political parties, during the early 1940s the Honduran polity included very few viable organized groups—the Tegucigalpa Chamber of Commerce, the University Student Federation, and perhaps the Catholic church. Since the early 1950s, a baffling array of groups, organizations, and new political movements has appeared. The first successful labor unions emerged only after the nationwide strike in 1954.

Coincidentally, the proliferation of new groups and organized political interest groups was paralleled by a sporadic, but significant, decline in the traditional party system. Permeated with outmoded visions and the legacy of caudillo politics, the parties failed to devise programs with which to confront the problems of national development. Despite the claim of support from all social classes (*policlasista*), the National and Liberal parties did little to integrate new participants into their ranks.

The Honduran political system has developed few, if any, political institutions that might integrate disparate social and economic interests. Military perspectives and institutions can impose order and authority, but they are not optimally suited as broker organizations. After more than a decade of military rule, the Honduran polity might be described as being in a state of "unstable immobilism in which governments changed but the political problems remained the same."[1] These problems have been (1) persistent demands for economic and social reform plus an effective, honest public administration; and (2) pressures for wider political participation patterns.

74

THE HISTORICAL PARTIES

For many observers, the two historical political parties appear much the same. Both parties incorporate similar values, have indistinctive political perspectives, and represent the interests of landed elites and the agribusiness-commercial classes. However, political experience and historical dynamics have created certain differences and images.

The Liberal Party of Honduras (PLH) has had to contend with the forces of internal division since its inception in 1890. Factionalism has been a fact of Liberal politics, and the party has tended to be less disciplined than its rival. With exiled leadership, and separated from public resources or patronage, the morale and organization of the Liberal party has suffered. The Liberals were revived under the leadership of nationally popular Dr. Ramón Villeda Morales, whose energy and ambition extended into the party rank and file. But the repressive military coup of 1963 shattered Liberal confidence, undermined the scarcely rebuilt party organization, and dispersed its leaders once again into exile. Beginning with the 1980s, the Liberals have been controlled by the Rodista wing of the party—more conservative followers of Modesto Rodas Alvarado, who succeeded Villeda Morales as party leader. Roberto Suazo Córdova carries on the mystique of *rodismo* (the body of principles or political philosophy advocated by Rodas) as the conservative mainstream of Liberal party doctrine.

Liberal party bylaws provide for the recognition and registration of distinct philosophical currents within the party. The only official faction is the left-of-center Popular Liberal Alliance (ALIPO), which has been important in past elections and will be critical in retaining popular-sector support for the party as a whole. ALIPO has no representation on the party's central committee and has gained little gratitude for its campaign and electoral activity. A new centrist faction was hastily organized in 1980 by dissident Liberals, including Dr. Ramón Villeda Bermúdez (son of the former president). The Liberal Unity Front (FUL) was initially rebuffed in its attempt to register as a full-fledged Liberal party faction.

Excessive factionalism, erratic leadership, and low morale did not afflict the National Party of Honduras (PNH) once it had been forged into a highly disciplined, well-integrated political organization under Tiburcio Carías Andino. However, party discipline faltered once Carías left office; a split developed between Carías and his former vice-president, Abraham Williams Calderón, who formed dissident followers into the National Reformist Movement (MNR). The split contributed to the indecisive electoral results of 1954 and the National party loss to the Liberals in 1957.

The PNH survived very well under the leadership of Ricardo Zúñiga Augustinius; his political intrigues helped to maintain the party's discipline, and he cultivated close relations with the conservative factions within the armed forces. In 1963, Zúñiga offered his services and the organization of his party to Colonel López Arellano. With behind-the-scenes maneuvering he was successful in keeping the Nationalists in the forefront during the National Unity government of 1971–1972.

Signs of organizational and political decay are present in both of the historical parties. In the aftermath of the 1980 and 1981 setbacks, Nationalist factions such as the Democratic Nationalist Forces and the Movement of Unity and Change pressured the leadership to expand organizational participation and restimulate the party's grass roots. The momentum of National party renovation accelerated after the disastrous loss in 1981, raising questions whether Zúñiga A. could hold his position at the head of the party. Indeed, by late 1983 it appeared that Zúñiga A. had been eased aside through intraparty maneuvering and behind-the-scenes alliances made by leaders of the Movement of Unity and Change. The Liberal party had won in areas that had been pockets of Nationalist support for decades. On the other hand, the Liberal party has suffered from a lack of dynamic leadership since the death of Modesto Rodas Alvarado. And although Roberto Suazo Córdova and the Liberals have made some accommodations with the military governors, little has been gained in return. Meanwhile, the youthful activists and progressive wings of the party have been relegated to the fringes of the organization.

The historical parties of Honduras are facing new realities with outmoded perspectives, and they have been bypassed with other channels of political communication. Regardless, they are not destined to simply wither away. For one thing, status quo interests, economic opportunity, and political stability act as common bonds among the traditional parties and forces. In addition, both the National and Liberal parties have extensive organizational networks that have functioned remarkably well, whether for higher or lower principles. Of course neither party has ever been seriously threatened by new political movements. The challenge by the Innovation and Unity party and the Christian Democrats has been minimal, despite the criticisms thrown at the traditional elites who control the historical parties.

OTHER PARTIES AND MOVEMENTS

New political parties must overcome formidable obstacles in order to thrive. For instance, the National and Liberal party elites do not relish prospects of serious competition from new political movements. The procedures for acquiring legal recognition (*personería jurídica*) are complex and at times subjectively administered. Finally, persistent voter loyalty has made proselytization of political converts difficult.

Even so, the forces of socioeconomic change and international influences affecting Honduran political development since 1950 have created new social strata and stimulated new levels of political awareness. The Innovation and Unity party (PINU) was first organized in 1970. In the wake of the 1969 war, after evaluating the deteriorating conditions in the country, concerned professionals decided to form a new political party. Led by Dr. Miguel Andonie Fernández, an independent businessman, PINU advocated policies to reduce economic and social inequities and expand participation in the political process. Despite the party's centrist position, it was not until 1979 that the Innovation and Unity party acquired legal status.

The Christian Democratic Party of Honduras (PDCH) is led by middle-class professionals and community activists. The party's ideology is a mixture of Christian ethics and social concern that places it to the left of center in the Honduran political spectrum. Origins of the PDCH are rooted in a series of development programs initially sponsored and/or supported by the Catholic church during the 1950s and 1960s. Activists involved in the creation of peasant leagues and several labor unions later became the core of a Christian social movement.[2] In 1975, a decision was made to reorganize as a political party and work toward gaining legal recognition. Denied recognition in 1978, the PDCH was unable to participate in the landmark 1980 Constituent Assembly elections. Subsequently, with revised conservative support, military acceptance, and pressures from the United States, legal recognition was granted the Christian Democrats later in 1980.

Another party of the democratic left is the Honduran Revolutionary party (PRH) formed by several peasant and labor leaders in 1977. Although not officially inscribed, the PRH is dedicated to expanding its base among workers and other sectors committed to change, effective suffrage, and citizen participation.[3] In the 1980 elections, the party supported independent candidates from Cortés department. Nevertheless, the PRH has failed to catch the imagination of a substantial number of Hondurans, and it is unlikely that the future bodes well for its survival as a significant political force.

The Communist Party of Honduras (PCH) was first established in 1927, reorganized in 1954, then declared illegal in 1957. The PCH has never been able to participate directly in elections. The old-line, pro-Moscow party has operated clandestinely and openly, but it recently has experienced serious divisions. A Marxist-Leninist faction was formed in 1971 (the Communist Party of Honduras–Marxist-Leninist or PCH-ML). The PCH supported the first phase of military rule in 1972, with its emphasis on agrarian reform and national development. During the latter part of the 1970s, some of its members were successful in winning control over several labor unions. Along with other leftist organizations the PCH became an active participant in the Honduran Patriotic Front (FPH).[4] Another party of the left is the Socialist Party (PASO) led by Marco Virgilio Carías. It likewise is not legally recognized and participated in the 1981 elections by offering independent candidates for the legislature.

The wave of systemic change in Central America—generated throughout most of the 1970s—was dramatically brought to a head in

1978 and 1979 with the success of the Sandinista-led revolution in Nicaragua. Violence in neighboring El Salvador exacerbated tensions within Honduras and made both the 1980 and 1981 elections that much more a counterpoint to events of the region.

Beyond the small, disorganized communist and socialist groups, extremist political movements had been noted mostly by their absence in contrast to those active in Guatemala and El Salvador. But regional conflicts have made an impact as refugees have fled to Honduras, and a variety of extremist groups have been stimulated into action. Communications among student, labor, and other popular sectors in Central America have led to the formation of numerous leftist fronts and ad hoc political-action cells. Several are offshoots of the Honduran Communist party and the Marxist-Leninist splinter group. Others are the product of longtime radical, or "professional," students with Marxist convictions. The Morazanist Front for the Liberation of Honduras (FMLH), the People's Revolutionary Union (URP), and the Cinchonero Popular Liberation Movement (MPL) were among several groups that made themselves known after 1978 and 1979.[5] Most are small and exist in name only. However, various actions modeled after events in other countries have taken place, such as the hijacking of a Honduran Air Services (SAHSA) airliner in March 1981 by the Cinchoneros. The most spectacular events were the bombings of electrical substations in the nation's capital city in July 1982 and the holding of more than one hundred hostages in the San Pedro Sula Chamber of Commerce building for several days in September.

NATIONAL INTEREST GROUPS

Since the 1940s, the number and diversity of political interest groups in Honduras has increased.[6] Most interest groups are organized along the lines of socioeconomic sectors. The pattern of national organizations has become even more complex as dissidents have split away to form rival associations. With the economy becoming more diversified, elements of the business community gradually recognized the need for some type of peak association to coordinate its strategies and monitor both domestic and international governmental policies that might affect commercial and industrial activity. Initiatives to set up the Honduran Council of Private Enterprise (COHEP) came from the San Pedro business community, the Cortés Chamber of Commerce (CCIC), and the Atlántida Chamber of Commerce (CCIA). COHEP was formally created in 1967 and is in fact an umbrella organization that includes most nationally organized private-sector associations. The several chambers of commerce, the National Association of Industries (ANDI), the Honduran Association of Banking and Insurance Institutions (AHIBA), and the National Federation of Agriculturists and Stockraisers of Honduras (FENAGH) share the important directorate. COHEP was a major force behind the proposal to the National and Liberal parties to form the National Unity government (the 1971–1972 Pacto). This action alienated the more conservative business sectors; when the Pacto agreement was reviewed in mid-1972, COHEP was represented at the sessions by two delegations. Formal unity was reestablished after 1973. However, rivalries and policy differences remain below the surface.

General Tiburcio Carías, as well as foreign and national employers, discouraged mobilization of workers; the formation of labor unions awaited a more conducive environment. The longest, most widespread, and perhaps only fully successful strike in Honduras began in May 1954, when dockworkers in Puerto Cortés refused to work on a religious holiday without overtime pay.[7] A Central Strike Committee began to coordinate the strike; the goverment either wavered or found itself unprepared to deal with the situation. Strikers sensed support among urban middle sectors and from among factions of the Liberal party. After two and a half months, a settlement was reached with the Tela Railroad Company. In August 1954, the Union of the Tela Railroad Company Workers (SITRATERCO) was formally organized.

The two largest labor confederations are the Confederation of Honduran Workers (CTH), affiliated with the Inter-American Regional Organization of Workers (ORIT); and the General Central of Workers (CGT), associated with the social-Christian-backed Latin American Central of Workers (CLAT). The ORIT-supported CTH has been more conservative in its approach to policy, seeking more immediate worker benefits rather than pushing for profound changes in the social and economic structure of Honduras. It also has maintained closer relations with most governments since its founding in 1964. The CTH is composed of two labor federations and an associated peasant movement: the Labor Federation of National Workers of Honduras (FESITRANH); the Central Federation of Free Worker Unions of Honduras (FECESITLIH) based in Tegucigalpa; and the National Association of Honduran Peasants (AN-ACH).

The more militant CGT was organized in 1970, and by the 1980s included several federations in its structure, such as the sugar workers, bank employee unions, and civil-service associations. The CGT's strength relies upon unions in Tegucigalpa and several in the southern part of Honduras, especially around Choluteca. But the strongest component of the CGT has been the active National Peasants Union (UNC), which claims a membership of around twenty-two thousand small and landless farmers. Though established later, in recent years the CGT has attracted several unions to its ranks from the larger and better financed CTH.

Although labor's political and economic strength cannot be ignored, its latitude of action depends in part on official tolerance. Organized labor can disrupt critical sectors of the economy (especially in the banana industry), but its ability to sustain a lengthy walkout is problematic. Moreover, past administrations and military governments have reacted with force to counteract strike activity. Another limitation is the small proportion of the economically active population (near 1.2 million) that is affiliated with either unions or peasant organizations.

During the 1950s, the Catholic church and other social activists directed their attention to the Honduran countryside. The church sponsored a series of religious revival meetings and Bible study groups and helped to establish Radio School literacy programs. This was also a period when idle lands began to be more widely exploited by agribusiness and large landholders. Small landowners and landless farmers were left to their own resources as the more traditional relationship between landlord and peasant was disrupted or broken completely. The church's appeal was in this case quite timely, in that a large portion of the rural population was in need of constructing new relations within the changing society.[8]

ANACH was first organized in 1962 in accordance with current labor laws. Total membership has ranged from 60,000 to 100,000 individuals and has shifted from mostly landless farmers to a membership with some land. In 1967, ANACH became part of CTH through its affiliation with the San Pedro Sula–based FESITRANH. This move helped attract more members, since it then had the support of the largest labor organization in Honduras. ANACH, legally recognized since 1963, generally has maintained close relations with the past several governments.

UNC has been the principal competitor of ANACH since the latter part of the 1960s. Repression after the 1963 coup, along with difficulties in attaining legal recognition by the military-backed regimes, hindered its ability to attract members. The UNC groups, or *ligas*, were originally associated with several of the rural programs sponsored by the Catholic church and activists of the Christian Democratic social movement. After 1970, the UNC emphasized its independence and became part of CGT.

A third peasant group is the Federation of Agrarian Reform Cooperatives of Honduras (FECORAH), a collection of independent associations originally established on lands acquired through the National Agrarian Institute (INA). Efraín Díaz Galeas, a former ANACH leader, organized these cooperatives into FECORAH during 1968. In 1974, the umbrella organization received its legal recognition. INA has lent technical assistance, and other cooperatives that had been set up by the institute have since joined the federation.

Since 1979, most peasant groups have lent their support to a National Unity Front of Honduran Peasants (FUNACAMPH). This informal structure, intended to strengthen political leverage on national issues of agrarian reform, was preceded by several tentative efforts to create a broader-based, more unified peasant movement. The most important attempt was in 1975 when UNC, ANACH, and FECORAH sank their more immediate differences in order to confront the central government in a unified fashion. FUNACAMPH initially grouped together the more militant splinter groups. ANACH, then led by Reyes Rodríguez, stayed aloof. But once the anti-Rodríguez faction gained control in 1980, ANACH leaders shifted their support to the Unity Front. The front was considered useful for common objectives, but the member groups continued to work independently toward their particular goals.

The peasant movement never has been politically unified. In part, this is a result of the distinctive origins of the principal groups and the tendency of Hondurans to ally themselves with one or the other of the historical political parties. In recent years organizational competition and other external influences have resulted in more factionalization. New groups have split off from ANACH and UNC. Other peasant organizations have sprung up out of the increasingly diverse rural sector. No one factor is sufficient to explain this phenomenon, but struggles have erupted over complacent leadership, issues of corruption, and a failure to produce adequate responses from Honduran authorities.

OTHER GROUPS AND THE CHURCH

Among the urban population, social and civic life is replete with associations and groups. Many of these are seldom active as political interest groups, but frequently they may take actions or issue statements intended to influence the behavior of government officials or affect policy formulation. Most can be categorized as professional (*colegios*) or social-service groups. Teachers are effectively organized, though independently of the labor movement. The various associations of elementary and secondary teachers are particularly important when it comes to education issues and working conditions for their members.[9]

A grass-roots type of organization that evolved during the 1970s is the community association, or *patronatos*. Most are set up to help citizens with government contacts, provide family training, and—in the case of rural associations—work toward the recuperation of *ejidal* lands. Demonstrations are organized, especially in the larger urban areas, to protest rising consumer prices or the lack of public services such as transport, water and sewerage facilities, or health clinics. Often, demonstrations are scheduled for the early morning hours when commuter traffic is heaviest and tempers are perhaps most fragile.

The Honduran Catholic church never has been wealthy or closely allied with the political or economic elites. The 1876 Liberal reforms took much away from the church; by the late 1920s, it had entered into a period of decline that lasted more than thirty years. The 1954 North Coast labor strike, the impact of Castro's revolution in Cuba, and a growing challenge by Protestant missionaries were all perceived as potential threats to the Catholic church. From the late 1950s until 1975, the church regenerated itself, and its social role helped influence the dynamics of the Honduran political system during the post-Carías years.[10]

A Radio School program was introduced to promote literacy in rural areas. The network of monitors and classes evolved into a "radio school movement" based on community involvement. Schools were placed under the sponsorship of the nonprofit Honduran Popular Cultural Action Agency (ACPHO) in 1963, and the government provided an annual fifteen-thousand-dollar subsidy. By 1964, more than fourteen thousand students were participating in 750 classes throughout the country.

A religious revival movement, including Bible teachers and urban-based courses in Christianity, gradually merged with the community-development facets of the church's pastoral activities. A coalition of rural peasants, church leaders, and urban, middle-class activists became the core of new political forces in Honduras during the 1960s and 1970s—UNC and PDCH. After eight peasants were killed at Talanquera in 1972, the church grew concerned over its continued association with the militant Christian Social Movement. Conservatives accused the church hierarchy of instigating land invasions, even though it no longer had any direct association or control over most of the community-action programs.

The church's role was elemental and timely in the rise of the rural peasant movement. Its efforts in community development and social action helped to develop new social relations and means of political expression; its intervention contributed toward a dispersal of power held by traditional political elites. The Catholic hierarchy had transformed itself into a rural-oriented *campesino*, or peasant, church. Church-sponsored social-service agencies, grouped together under the Coordinating Council for Development (CONCORDE), had become strong enough to compete successfully with government agencies in responding to and meeting the needs of rural citizens. Along with the various community structures and the derived national networks, alternative channels of political articulation had been forged.

After 1975, the church pulled back from the forefront of community activism in order to avoid political persecution. Seeking to depoliticize itself, it left incomplete the potential phenomenon of solid grass-roots participation in the polity. A cautionary low profile was maintained even while customary pastoral duties were still performed. But social concern was slowly revived when violence escalated within Central America and the Honduran economy entered a downturn. Worsening economic conditions and the prospect of national elections in 1980 caused some of the clergy to criticize the absence of political vision among political leaders. In response, military governors implied that the church still harbored currents of opinion that could lead to social unrest.

The turn of events had forced the church into a difficult position. Its pastoral obligation was to help establish the dignity of its parishioners. This could be accomplished only if citizens were able to attain self-confidence, organize, and participate fully in society. But efforts to develop a broader social awareness threatened the traditional political elites. Those who controlled Honduras directly or indirectly impeded politicization of individuals and groups, labeling those who dared to think and organize themselves differently than the traditional political parties as bad, subversive, or communist.[11]

THE MILITARY

The armed forces of Honduras are a new institution that developed an efficient, professional organization only after World War II. Honduran military forces often resembled guerrilla bands or were merely armed supporters of aspirant presidential candidates. Beginning with the 1940s, a series of agreements with the United States provided training and equipment and inspired the organization of a professional armed force in Honduras.[12] The U.S. Military Mission assisted in setting up the "Francisco Morazán" Military School, which now serves as the principal source of new officers. Honduran military personnel received further training either in the United States or at the School of the Americas in the Panama Canal Zone. By 1969, over one thousand Hondurans had gone through a variety of courses in U.S. training facilities.[13]

Training and organization have contributed to a growing institutional identity among the armed forces of Honduras. Training resources have expanded, with officers traveling to European countries and attending schools in Brazil, Argentina, and Peru. Emissaries from Argentina and Chile have advised the army and police units. Another facet of professionalization was added in 1981 with the establishment of a Command and General Staff School (Escuela de Comando y Estado Mayor). Institutional identity was bolstered by the military code first legislated in 1970 and revised in 1975.[14]

Since 1957, the Honduran military has maintained a substantial autonomy vis-à-vis civilian authority. The 1957 and 1965 constitutions included provisions that, though recognizing the president of the republic as commander-in-chief, placed direct command in the hands of the armed forces' senior officers. And it was through the head of the armed forces that the president was to exercise his constitutional authority. Moreover, any disputes or disagreements with a presidential order would be submitted to the National Congress for resolution. The head of the armed forces was formerly chosen by the Congress for a six-year term. In 1982, the term was changed to five years (the president and the congress served four years). The final selection of the head of the armed forces is made from a list submitted to the Congress by the Superior Council of the Armed Forces (CONSUFFAA). The president names the minister of defense, but the cabinet-level position is only administrative and has no direct command over active military units.

The military has come of age and has been directly involved in politics, but internal frictions and rivalries have been generated. Even so, without the burdens of historical memory, intraservice competition has been kept to minimal levels. More of a problem has been the differing perspectives between older and younger officers. New officers acquired expertise and exposure through training and international travels, and they soon became impatient with their more tradition-oriented superiors. One of the first signs was the easing aside of Gen. Roque Rodríguez, who ostensibly had led the first military intervention in 1956.

Excepting the brief period of reformism (1972–1975), pressures to retire senior officers generally are not ideological but rather are derived from the competition for promotion, power, and access to economic opportunities. The involvement of General López Arellano in the United Brands scandal has been emulated on a lesser scale by participation of some CONSUFFAA members in bribery, dubious business connections, kickbacks on government contracts, and smuggling of arms, cattle, and other contraband, not to mention the sensitive topic of drug trafficking.

Factionalism within the Honduran military reached its apogee sometime between 1969 and 1975. Retirements and transfers rid the ranks of dissident officers while opening the ranks for promotion and advancement. The status of the traditional political elites was revived when it was judged that the military's interests were protected. Those interests became more economic as members of the high command availed themselves of opportunities afforded to them as governors or proposed to them by willing civilian collaborators. In some respects, the colonels followed the example of their general, López Arellano.

The armed forces of Honduras became rulers under conditions of rapid social and economic change, unresolved shifts in political realignment, and new global relations. The disintegration of traditional social ties and mobilization during the 1950s and 1960s coincided with the decline or stagnation of traditional political institutions. The polity had little precedent, other than the authoritarian and personalistic rule of Carías, that might have provided some guide to integration of the polity. The political vacuum was gradually filled by the more confident military institution, which became less and less enchanted of civilian politicians and their ability to govern.

Economic development problems and the threat of social chaos stimulated the search for an orderly and effective means of governing. The technocrats became new allies of their military counterparts within a situation of few political constraints. The administration of national development policy was to be based on political stability and efficient planning and without the complicating aspects of "politics." These goals were achieved in part by the emergence of CONSUFFAA into policy-making and later into controlling policy implementation through the Regional Development Councils.

Despite the establishment of military rule, the stresses of governing demonstrated that the armed forces were not immune to civilian political influences—especially the more entrenched conservative sectors. General López Arellano had shifted his political base onto a small body of technocrats, some of the new entrepreneurial groups, and the (at times) hesitant labor and peasant movements. But even though the traditional political sectors were stagnant, they had not disappeared. In short, the civil-military linkages oriented around the National party and the conservative ranching interests regained some of their customary influence. Pressures of governing amid an at times strident opposition aggravated differences within the military institution. And these differences were employed by the civilian sectors in order to promote their own narrow interests. One of those was the return to "constitutional" rule at the beginning of the 1980s.

7

The Economy and National Development Policy

Agriculture—whether subsistence, commercial, or export-oriented—is the basis of the Honduran economy. Most of the population is employed in the agrarian sector, and the bulk of the country's foreign exchange is acquired by exporting bananas, coffee, wood, and meat. Since 1950, substantial industrial growth has occurred with that sector now contributing 17–20 percent of the country's gross domestic product. A similar expansion of the public sector's economic role has evolved through infrastructure investments, monetary and fiscal policies, planning, and the establishment of new government agencies.

The Honduran economy has grown and diversified in the face of persistent obstacles. Hurricanes periodically batter the North Coast region with heavy winds and precipitation. Every few years drought causes crop failure and lower yields. The war with El Salvador, difficulties within the Central American Common Market, and the impact of the Central American crisis during the 1980s have brought further burdens upon the economy. Despite growth and diversity, Honduras remains dependent upon the export of primary products for its national livelihood. It also relies upon the import of capital goods, raw materials, technology, and petroleum supplies that are vital to the nation's continued industrial and agribusiness expansion. In many respects, the economic fortunes of Honduras turn upon the nexus between export capacity and import needs. During the late 1970s and early 1980s, rising energy prices, high interest rates, and more expensive capital goods combined with deteriorating world market conditions to create higher cost-price ratios. The overall impact was to increase trade and balance-of-payment deficits and to expand the demand for external financing. Thus, in recent years, Honduras has been swept up in the vicious cycle of rising national and foreign debt just as income generation has weakened.

THE ECONOMY

The agrarian nature of the Honduran economic base and its reliance upon exports were established early, as mining and cattle raising historically affected land-use patterns and the structure of social development. Liberal reform governments of the late 1870s and early 1880s encouraged acquisition and exploitation of larger land units and provided import and tax concessions that, for the most part, were granted to foreign investors. By the 1930s, the banana export industry was preponderant and the mold of export dependency had been well established.

The dual nature of Honduran agriculture and society (traditional and modern), though over a century old, became a critical political issue after 1950. Economic diversification, greater demands for commodities, expanded exports, availability of credit, and other international linkages helped to stimulate industrial growth and a more dynamic commercial-agribusiness sector. This breaking out of the modern "enclave" economy (essentially the North Coast) affected land use and led to conflicts over tenancy in the countryside. Over the last three and a half decades, a growing governmental apparatus has been confronted with competing demands from private landowners, aspiring industrial and financial investors, an organized working class, and the emergent peasant movement. Issues and policy decisions have revolved about priorities of social reform and land distribution versus economic infrastructure development and wider exploitation of the country's natural resources.

Agriculture and Industry

Although today most of the Honduran population labors in subsistence agriculture, more than three-quarters of all Honduran export income is derived from commercial-agribusiness operations. The economic impact of the banana industry has declined in relative terms as other commodities now compete for export markets. The original investments of the banana corporations have been diversified into manufacturing, chemical production, and stock raising. Foreign influence is still a fact of life, but its presence is less visible and more difficult to pinpoint as the interests of domestic and foreign investors have become more intertwined.[1]

However, Honduras still gains 25–28 percent of its export income from banana sales, and a hurricane or plant disease can drastically alter the national budget and the income of several thousand workers. Along with beef, lumber, and coffee, banana and fruit production represent the semi-industrialized, export-oriented agricultural sector. A point to emphasize here is the "dependence" of Honduras upon the agricultural export sector for a major share of its foreign exchange and a substantial portion of its gross domestic product.

The urban-technical elite has allied itself with foreign investment and technology without requiring any change in the backward structure of subsistence production within which most of the Honduran population lives and works.[2] The relevance of this traditional agrarian sector is illustrated by the distribution of the economically active population (EAP). Even though 60 percent of the labor force is engaged in agricultural or primary production, only a small proportion is employed in commercial agriculture. If children younger than ten years were included in the EAP, the population involved in agriculture would surpass 70 percent.

The low productivity and backwardness of traditional agriculture is emphasized when distribution of the labor force is compared with sectoral economic production figures. Table 2.1, though simplified, showed that even in 1980 most of the EAP produced less than half of the gross domestic product. The three decades since 1950 had brought relatively little change to some aspects of the Honduran rural economy.

Changes in the labor force have occurred slowly but steadily since 1950, when 84 percent of the labor force was engaged in fishing, lumbering, and for the most part subsistence agriculture and only 5 percent was classed as part of the manufacturing sector. Eleven years later, industry accounted for 11 percent of the labor force; by the end of 1980, the figure was 17 percent. The change leveled off after the initial growth of industry, since newer enterprises were more capital intensive than labor intensive. The stimulus to internal migration and the growth of urban centers have expanded the tertiary service sector with disguised underemployment.

Industrial production during the first part of the 1960s contributed 13 percent toward Honduran exports. With a small base, industrial growth was rapid at first, but it began to stabilize by the end of the decade. Limited infrastructure, an underskilled labor force, and a relatively inexperienced entrepreneurial class were the principal constraints. A more attractive industrial base in other Central American countries, especially Guatemala and El Salvador, made competition and survival difficult for Honduran businesses. The private sector was unaccustomed to direct competition. Technology had only begun to be applied in the exploitation of Honduran resources, and many regions were still unexplored or untouched. In several instances, resources were inefficiently utilized. The prevalence of the provincial "captive market" attitude among the newer industrial elite was compounded by an absence of any development-oriented political leadership until the 1970s.

The bulk of Honduran industry is made up of sugar refining, flour milling, textile production, beverage and food processing, and the manufacturing of light consumer goods such as clothing and wood products. Secondary production includes chemicals, petroleum derivatives, and cement. By the end of the 1980s, a long-dreamed-of pulp and paper mill should be operating in the forest reserve of Olancho. A second cement plant of 1,000-ton-per-day capacity came on line in 1981 near Potrerillos, Cortés; a steel plant has been proposed, but Honduras has few hydrocarbon deposits suitable for siderurgical activities.

Main headquarters for Banco Atlántida—the largest bank in Honduras.

Most Honduran manufacturing depends upon imports for much of its capital equipment needs, raw materials, technology, and some financing. Including transportation and fuels, nearly 80 percent of all Honduran imports are destined for industrial use or benefit.[3] Almost three-quarters of the industrial capacity is located in and around San Pedro Sula and the capital city. The department of Atlántida also has a high proportion of industrial activity. These areas are the core of the central zone "development corridor," and they are focuses of attraction within the national pattern of rural-urban migration.

Government and Industry

Previously, government support for industry was mostly indirect, consisting of minor tariff revisions to help stimulate import substitution. There was also heavy reliance upon foreign investment and imported technology. Pres. Tiburcio Carías Andino (1932–1949), besides being politically conservative, was economically unsophisticated; it was only when his successor, Juan Manuel Gálvez (1950–1954), was in office that new economic institutions and policies were introduced.

It was not until 1950 that the Central Bank of Honduras was established. Similarly, the National Development Bank was set up to provide credit for agriculture and industry alike. Before 1950 the Banco Atlántida, first organized in 1912 by the Standard Fruit and Steamship Company, in effect acted as the country's primary monetary institution by issuing bills of credit and facilitating foreign transactions. Standard Fruit and United Fruit both granted loans to various administrations throughout the first part of the twentieth century. The lempira was not established as the Honduran national unit of currency until 1926; North American currency circulated freely until the end of World War II because of continued shortages of coinage.[4] The Central Bank of Honduras and the National Development Bank subsequently took on the tasks of conducting monetary policy, controlling credit, and making foreign exchange available.

Economic growth and development led to a rapid expansion of banking after 1967 as both nationally owned and foreign institutions multiplied. The Central American Common Market, industrial development, and new growth in the banana industry coincided with a general expansion of international banking. It was at this time that foreign economic interests consolidated their financial position in Honduras. In 1965 and 1966, 50 percent of Banco Atlántida, though already a foreign-owned bank, was purchased by Chase Manhattan Bank. First National City Bank acquired majority interest in the Banco de Honduras, and the Bank of America initiated its Tegucigalpa operations about the same time. By 1972, nearly two-thirds of the country's branch offices were represented by foreign-owned or -controlled institutions.[5] Other foreign-owned savings institutions, insurance companies, and banks held among them one-third of the country's assets. Expanded financial and credit facilities were, and continue to be, necessary to the Honduran strategy of development; but the extent of foreign involvement in the country's financial sector, along with the dependence on exports, indicates that development will remain influenced by decisions and policies made in the industrially advanced nations of North America and Europe.

Despite the creation of official banks, lack of capital and credit and basic infrastructure problems plagued the economy, and industrial entrepreneurs were left to finance their own expansion and maintain working capital levels. The government saw little reason to provide incentives until 1958, when the Liberal administration of Ramón Villeda Morales (1957–1963) responded to pressures with passage of an Industrial Development Law. Technical aid and credit were made available to those industrial projects that met internal demand or increased Honduran export capacity. Incentives included a reduced income tax and exemptions for capital investment and export taxes, and certain primary and construction materials were freed from import duties. Between 1960 and 1971, 340 businesses were certified under the 1958 law.[6] Nevertheless, Honduran industry did not expand or diversify like that of some of the country's common market partners.

Economic Crisis

Besides the regional political conflict, the 1980s brought to Honduras and other Central American countries severe economic deterioration.

The economic crisis was fueled by a combination of world recession; falling prices for coffee, bananas, meat, wood, and other primary export products; and a generalized shortage of credit. This was compounded by rising fiscal deficits, a flight of capital, and inflation. Economic growth in Honduras entered into a sharp downturn in 1980; the gross domestic product declined as levels of investment and export income dropped.

After stagnation during the mid-1970s, the latter part of the decade was a period of dynamic economic growth in Honduras. World prices of the country's principal commodity exports were rising, and coffee had finally become a significant export crop. In fact, coffee surpassed bananas as the leading export earner in 1977 and 1978, amounting to one-third of the total income (see Fig. 7.1). Higher national income in turn facilitated an expansion of public-sector investment designed to increase the nation's productive infrastructure.

But the economic crisis decreased considerably the government's ability to finance and implement its national development policies. Reduced bank deposits, capital flight, less lending by international banks, and fiscal deficits all contributed to a credit shortage. Between 1977 and 1981, it is estimated that over $1 billion left Honduras. The lempira had been maintained as a stable, freely convertible currency; as regional violence and political uncertainty spread after 1978, Hondurans and other Central Americans converted their savings into dollar accounts in the United States or Europe. Another stimulus to withdraw funds from the country was the prospect of a crackdown on corruption by the incoming Liberal administration of Roberto Suazo Córdova in early 1982.

Energy costs and higher import expenses exacerbated the economic slide. Petroleum amounted to nearly one-fifth of Honduran imports by value in the late 1970s and early 1980s. Even though Mexico and Venezuela instituted the "oil facility" in 1980, Honduras was unable to benefit at first due to conflicts with Texaco (which owns and operates the country's only refinery) over import terms and pricing. Almost three-fifths of the country's imports are primary products and supplies destined for the small manufacturing sector, and rising prices of these items inhibited the growth and competitiveness of Honduran companies.

Business failures accelerated during 1982. Fernando Lardizábal G., leader of the Honduran Council of Private Enterprise, indicated that most plants were operating at 50 percent of capacity. Rising costs, low cash flow, and inflation had forced cutbacks in production and furlough of employees. Indications were that about 56 percent of the labor force was either unemployed or underemployed. Again these rates tended to be higher in rural areas.

To fill the gap, the civilian government of Suazo Córdova was forced to expand its borrowing, and most of that had to come from international sources. In 1982, Honduras was successful in attracting $300 million in loans from multilateral agencies in addition to an increase

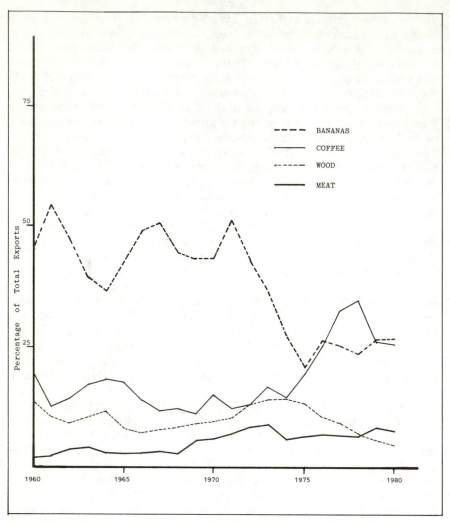

Figure 7.1   Composition of Major Honduran Exports by Value, 1960–1980

in aid from the United States. But also, from 1978 to 1982, the external public debt of Honduras rose from $600 million to more than $1.6 billion; service payments rose accordingly.

The price for obtaining international loans and additional credit was an obligation by the government to implement a series of economic austerity measures, a difficult course in any case, but especially so as the nation faced the stubborn problems of its national development. The International Monetary Fund required "austerity measures" (less government spending, monetary and fiscal policies designed to stimulate savings, investment, confidence) before approving balance-of-payment loans, "special drawing rights," or assets designed to aid Honduras in its cash-flow bind. Conservative business leaders and the U.S. embassy staff also encouraged similar policies. Stimulus and inducements for private investment were emphasized. The so-called Facusse Memorandum pressed for government to seek more foreign credits and investment, and it encouraged disestablishing several of the decentralized state agencies such as COHDEFOR and COHBANA.[7] These entities, as discussed in Chapters 4 and 5, had been created during the 1970s as state-led national development policies were implemented under the military governments. Tax reforms were recommended to alleviate part of the rising fiscal deficits. The sales tax was increased, and a 15 percent tax surcharge was placed upon upper-income groups. Budget expenditures were cut back, and public-sector investments were reduced. In addition, President Suazo Córdova decided to absorb debts incurred by several of the more inefficient and corruptly managed state agencies. The most serious problem was that of the National Investment Corporation (CONADI). Set up in 1974, it had incurred foreign debts of some $175 million; of its loans to domestic enterprises, fully a third were unable to be recovered. Rather than force more business closures, the central government had to assume many of CONADI's obligations.[8]

The mid- and late 1980s should bring a measure of relief to the country's economic crisis as the world economy recovers. Softened oil prices should also alleviate some of the external pressures and costs. Nevertheless, Honduras remains highly dependent upon external markets, world price fluctuations, and primary material imports for its economic well-being. The need for external credit, foreign private investment, and bilateral or multilateral financial and technical aid did not diminish but expanded rapidly during the 1970s. Measures to resolve the economic plight of Honduras have been undermined by the anxiety and uncertainty of revolution in Central America as well as by the ensuing struggle among other nations to influence its course, to be covered in the next chapter. Thus, to the country's economic crisis are added the pressures of regional geopolitics. Even under optimum conditions, any elected civilian government, or military government for that matter, would be faced with almost intractable problems of national development. As it is, during the 1980s and perhaps into the 1990s, the Central American drama of revolutionary conflict inhibits economic recovery in Honduras and severely tests the country's political stability.

NATIONAL DEVELOPMENT

The basic objective of Honduran economic policymakers since 1950 has been to create and expand the nation's infrastructure: roads, electricity, communications, financial institutions, and administrative capability. Infrastructure development, however, is dependent on foreign credits and assistance. And to successfully finance large projects, the nation's export capacity must be maintained if not actually expanded. In general, the agribusiness sector has been increasing its productivity. One example is the growth of banana exports even as fewer workers and less land are employed. On the other hand, credit shortages, bad weather, and the nature of subsistence agriculture (i.e., low production and productivity) have contributed to declines in harvests of basic grains—rice, sorghum, maize, beans. These food crops, central to the Honduran diet, are increasingly scarce and rising in price. Together with high population growth rates, the effect is to fuel inflation of basic food costs and undermine efforts to combat rural malnutrition.

With few exceptions, notably the Liberal government of Villeda Morales, civilian political leaders have failed to address critical administrative and political obstacles to national development. The National Unity government (1971–1972), under the terms of the Pacto agreement, had at least an implicit mandate for reform and active governmental programs, but the message was ignored. Popular-sector frustration and political tensions were vented somewhat during the "reformist" phase under López Arellano as the military-technocrat government launched several reforms, particularly those directed at the agrarian sector. Under military rule, the coalition of progressives—junior officers, North Coast business leaders, labor and peasant groups, some professionals—was dedicated to resolution of some of the country's more critical problems. Power had fallen into the hands of nontraditional leadership, which brought new attitudes to bear upon national development, attitudes that gave an impetus to distinct policies.

This new perspective and desire to surmount social and administrative barriers was embodied in a series of National Development Plans (NDPs). A 1974–1978 plan was followed by another (1979–1983) that contained similar principles and objectives. Incorporating long-term strategies, neither pretended to resolve the nation's problems in just a few years. In addition to basic transformation and nationalistic goals, the NDPs specified an "improved and intensified" role for the public sector. Specifically, the government would be responsible for creating conditions more conducive to development. Annual operative plans would detail goals, projects of physical and social infrastructure, and the modernization of public administration.

Exports are still the key to continued financing and international credits that provide the wherewithal to import equipment, technology, and other capital goods. Nearly 60 percent of the planned investment is destined for infrastructure projects—roads, hydroelectricity, port construction. Even though these will more than likely help future growth, the short-term economic growth rate may suffer as inflation, rising energy costs, and a still high population growth rate continue. These and other external factors will affect just how realistic Honduran development goals are and to what extent they will be achieved. Added to global economic trends is the Central American regional crisis that has shaken the confidence of both domestic and international investors.

The aspirations for new industrial development have been directed toward self-sufficiency in the production of electricity and the promise of an expanded forest and wood-product industry. In 1980, almost 60 percent of the generating capacity was provided by hydroelectric facilities with the remainder dependent upon imported fuels. A major expansion, however, is the highly touted El Cajón dam on the Rio Humuya that will bring an additional 292 megawatts on-line by the late 1980s. The project is designed for irrigation and flood control and most importantly, will enable Honduras to meet all its electricity needs.[9] Moreover, El Cajón supposedly will generate surplus energy that can be exported to other countries in Central America.

For nearly twenty-five years, technocrats and foreign corporations have gazed wistfully at the map of Olancho department envisioning the harvest of 1.5 million hectares of pine forests. National Development Plans have implied that nationally controlled development of the country's forest resources would help to increase and diversify Honduran exports. Just as the new industries would also provide a multiplier effect or stimulation to the nation's industrial sector, so too the roads and other facilities pushed into the wilderness would help populate the isolated eastern portion of the country. In 1974, the government nationalized all forests and set up the Honduran Forestry Development Corporation (COHDEFOR) to administer those resources. The Olancho project was finally launched after 1977 when the first loans were granted by the Inter-American Development Bank. The Honduran government has sponsored the Forest Industry Corporation of Olancho (CORFINO), which is to direct the fifteen-year operation.

The development of Olancho's forests is essential to more balanced economic growth. Indisputably it will add to the gross national product, create jobs, enhance exports, and stimulate associated industries. There are questions, however. Sawmill capacity may be overdesigned given the annual growth rates; if the mills are employed fully, the operation may contribute to further deforestation and subsequent soil erosion. Though seeding and reforestation programs are slated, it is another matter to implement them properly in conjunction with programmed resource exploitation. The widespread practice of slash-and-burn subsistence agriculture is still another factor that dims any real prospect of reversing forest losses.[10]

Land Tenure and the Agrarian Sector

Agriculture and the export of primary products form the base of the Honduran economy, and thus possession of the land is important for the political and economic elites as well as for the rural masses who need land for daily survival. The landed elite has manipulated and controlled a political system in which the rural subsistence farmer has barely participated. Arrival of the foreign-owned banana industry at the turn of the century did little to disrupt the nature of economic and political control. With concessions granted by the state, the fruit companies occupied the river valleys and the fertile littoral along the North Coast. The contemporary pattern of landholding is characterized by highly concentrated ownership, with a small number of individuals and corporations controlling extensive areas.

Acquisition of land was historically easy. It was not until after World War II, amidst changing socioeconomic conditions and mobilization of the rural classes, that land availability and agrarian reform became critical political issues. Economic growth during the 1950s and 1960s stimulated expansion and consolidation of other large landholdings. As the Honduran population has grown, relatively available land has become more difficult to acquire or more expensive to rent.

There have been three cadastral surveys since 1950. The data indicate that the "duality" of the Honduran agricultural sector has persisted despite migration to less populated areas, urbanization, colonization projects, or the more recent policies of land distribution conducted under the aegis of agrarian reform. In all cases, the small- and medium-sized farms composed over 95 percent of all units, yet they occupied less than half of the agricultural lands surveyed. On the other hand, 4 percent of the land units occupy well over half of the territory in production. The status of landholding patterns is actually worse than that presented by the figures in Table 7.1: within the O–5 hectare category, most landholdings are concentrated below 2 hectares; the average size of a holding at this level has declined since 1952.[11]

Agrarian Reform Policies, 1962–1980

Agrarian reform as a concept encompasses much more than the redistribution or partition of land. Simple land distribution does not solve national production or productivity problems nor does it guarantee an improvement in the situation of the recipient farmer. Credit, agricultural extension work, new methods of cultivation, education, community development, and basic infrastructure such as roads, marketing facilities, and cooperatives must eventually accompany any fully successful partition of lands. There is little argument about the broader concept of agrarian reform despite the immense difficulties and expense inherent in any effective program. Nevertheless, the salient and most pertinent issue to both the large landholder and landless laborer is the simple possession of land. With it, the owner of large rural estates (*latifundista*) assures future wealth, status, and power. Without it, the peasant has less chance for survival. The issue of agrarian reform in Honduras begins with land, and most political activity is directed at defending its possession or acquiring it.

Early efforts at agrarian reform generally failed because there were few conditions present to support their success. Before 1960 there were

TABLE 7.1
Number and Area of Agricultural Holdings by Size, 1974

Size of Holding		Number	%	Area (in hectares)	%	Average Size of Holding (in hectares)
0-4.9	Hectares	124,781	63.9	238,993	9.1	1.9
5-49.9	"	62,654	32.1	930,635	35.4	14.9
50-499.9	"	7,461	3.8	881,132	33.5	118.1
500 and over	"	445	0.2	579,099	22.0	1,301.3
Republic		195,341	100.0	2,629,859	100.0	13.46

Source: Dirección General de Estadística y Censos, Censo nacional agropecuario, 1974. Vol. 2, Tenencia de la tierra. Ministerio de Economía, Tegucigalpa, D.C., September 1978, p. 2.

no active peasant associations to press for the initiation of such programs or to help implement them once started. A more elemental factor was the lack of national communications, distribution problems, and deficient credit facilities. Even more important was the absence of any serious political decision to push ahead with effective agrarian reform. Generally, Honduran political leadership has either avoided the difficult decisions or acted to defuse tensions through stopgap measures, legal maneuvering, or repression.

The 1962 Agrarian Reform Law was passed by the National Congress as the consequence of increasing domestic and international pressures.[12] Without those pressures, it is questionable whether even the Liberal government of Ramón Villeda Morales would have devised the comprehensive program. The 1961 Inter-American Conference at Punta del Este formally committed the American nations to an Alliance for Progress based on higher levels of foreign and domestic investment coupled with internal social and political reforms on the part of Latin Americans. Reform laws were deemed necessary before the United States and other international sources would provide development loans and grants. The 1962 Agrarian Reform Law in Honduras was among similar laws passed in several Central American and South American republics in response to the program espoused by the United States. Once the need to develop some type of systematic land reform was finally realized, the National Agrarian Institute (INA) was created in March 1961 to administer and oversee land distribution, propose colonization projects, and organize rural cooperatives. Any progress in land reform that might have been intended by the Liberal government was precluded by the October 1963 coup that placed Colonel López Arellano in power. The effect upon the peasant movement was drastic, as rural activism was repressed. INA experienced changes in its personnel, and its budget was reduced to a point at which it hardly exceeded administrative expenses. Resistance to effective land-reform policies continued until the late 1960s, when the dormant peasant movement was revived.

Market and production factor changes during the 1960s induced more intensive and more profitable land use, and landowners enclosed formerly idle lands and occupied national lands, fencing them for grazing and evicting the subsistence farmer. The methods employed varied from shifts of title through political influence and bribery to outright illegal occupation of national and *ejidal* lands. All of this was happening in the face of rapid population increases in Honduras. The two southern departments of Valle and Choluteca already formed one of the more densely populated areas, and pressures upon the land in that region increased tremendously after 1955. The land rental price rose, squeezing the peasant even more. Many landowners now wanted the rent in advance before any crops had been produced. Waves of evictions increased the numbers of landless farmers, and separation from the land produced a certain degree of anomie and alienation. Perhaps by fortune, the rural-focused programs of the Catholic church were well under way by the late 1960s.

In 1968 and 1969, the revived peasant movement changed strategies and began to pressure the central government. Land occupations (or invasions) had been frequent, but from 1969 to 1973 they increased in number and became more widespread.[13] Invasions were considered a last resort, but the only effective means that would force INA to act upon the demands of the peasants. It was this "creation of crisis" that became the means of getting landholder, government, and other parties together with the peasant to resolve the situation at hand.

There had been general expectations that the National Unity government of 1971-1972 would begin to act forcefully on rural-sector problems. Its failure to address some of the demands articulated by the peasant movement only served to widen the gap of alienation between government and the peasant movement. With the December 1972 military coup, the political balance of power had shifted temporarily toward the now dominant "reformist" factions within the armed forces that had formed an implicit alliance with Honduran popular sectors. This alliance had its origins prior to the 1969 war with El Salvador, when North Coast business and labor leaders had become preoccupied about the country's near total economic stagnation.[14] López Arellano was also obligated to the organized peasant movement because of its instrumental role in the 1972 coup. On 26 December 1972, Decree Law No. 8 was issued, providing for the forced rental of lands or transfer of idle private lands for up to two years.

The law was recognized as a stopgap measure to lessen the prospect of agrarian conflict. During the two-year life envisioned for Decree Law No. 8, the military government was to design a more permanent National Plan of Agrarian Reform. Land invasions continued—out of desperation and as a pressure tactic. It must have seemed to the landed elites as though anarchy, aided by the state, was about to consume traditional Honduran society. INA officials processed applications for land in six regional offices. When Decree Law No. 8 expired in January 1975, INA had facilitated 632 settlements (asentamientos) involving some 109,000 manzanas and benefiting nearly twenty-four thousand families. Only half the settlements were made on private land; the rest were made on communal (ejidal), national or mixed-tenancy lands.[15]

A year after López Arellano had presented his fifteen-year National Development scheme, the long-awaited 1975 Agrarian Reform Law was issued. The scope of agrarian reform was outlined, and the definition of the "social function" of land was clarified. Cattle ranchers were required to intensify production. Small farmers who held 5 hectares of land were not eligible under auspices of the agrarian-reform program. The property of all landholders would be limited to from 100 to 1,500 hectares depending on terrain, fertility, and type of production. On the other hand, if adequately exploited, those lands producing commercial export crops—bananas, sugarcane, coffee, citrus—were exempted from the appropriation sections of the law. As predicted, those settlements made under Decree Law No. 8 were ratified, and titles officially transferred to the occupants.

Though decreed early in the year, difficulties in formulating appropriate regulations postponed any implementation of the Agrarian Reform Law to the last half of 1975. The timing of this delay was unfortunate, since it occurred prior to the annual planting season. Rural impatience ran up against bureaucratic indifference, which forced peasant-movement leaders once again to consider land invasions as a pressure tactic. The mid-1975 protests were met firmly by Melgar Castro and the Superior Council of the Armed Forces. Shortly thereafter, the tragic events of "Los Horcones" unraveled in Olancho.

The amount of land distributed under the agrarian laws since 1962 has not been impressive. INA's task has been hampered by political constraints, budgetary limitations, massive paperwork, and complicated legal procedures. Only 16 percent of the land distributed between 1962 and 1980 was awarded prior to 1973. The high point was reached during the 1973–1975 life of Decree Law No. 8 when just over half of the territory was adjudicated (Table 7.2). This "reformist" phase of military government was followed by the conservative backlash, and the amounts of land distributed annually tumbled to pre-1969 levels. After two decades of official commitment to land distribution and agrarian reform, the reformed or contemporary sector of Honduran agriculture constituted only 9 percent of all holdings surveyed in 1973–1974. The Suazo government claimed to have distributed nearly 25,000 hectares in 1982 or double the rate of distribution during the last two years of military rule. Regardless, financial constraints continued to plague the Suazo government and the budget of the INA suffered accordingly.

Agrarian reform policy since 1975 has preserved and extended the modern subsector of agricultural production. The form of land grants, the pattern of credit, and encouragement of cash-crop production—the bulk of it destined for export—has left much of the basic grain production in the hands of subsistence farmers whose productivity is limited by a lack of credit and marketing facilities and by poor farming methods. The policy bias has been toward increasing market production, restraining the "push" aspects of urban migration, and defusing rural discontent. Regardless, high population growth rates, rising numbers of landless poor, and deficient basic grain supplies all will serve to keep the dilemma of agrarian reform versus the demands of commercial export production very much in the forefront of Honduran political issues.

Revised Banana Policies

The mid-1970s were traumatic years for agrarian policy and the Honduran economy as a whole. The destructive 1974 hurricane Fifi had struck the North Coast, affecting the nation's export base, particularly

TABLE 7.2
Land Distribution and Settlements in Honduran
Agrarian Reform, 1962-1980

Year of Settlement	Number of Settlements	Number of Actual Families	Total Land Awarded (hs)
1962	2	27	281
1963	4	57	447
1964	2	48	194
1965	2	72	154
1966	2	77	281
1967	4	294	2,477
1968	7	326	1,670
1969	22	886	5,735
1970	26	890	6,386
1971	34	1,553	7,751
1972	72	1,399	10,585
1973	224	4,663	32,454
1974	287	7,076	47,098
1975	186	5,941	37,252
1976	182	4,266	26,913
1977	106	2,198	15,985
1978	80	1,515	4,224
1979	99	2,342	9,855
1980	77	2,842	16,713
Total	1,418	36,472	226,455

Source: Instituto Nacional Agrario, Departamento de Planificación, Tegucigalpa, D.C., 1981.

in the case of bananas. Conflicts among peasant groups, conservative ranchers, and government authorities exacerbated rural tensions and nationwide recovery efforts. Then, the 1975 bribery scandal involving the United Brands transnational corporation and high government officials, besides triggering the ouster of General López Arellano, precipitated revision of national policy toward banana production and official relations with the foreign-owned companies.

Earlier in 1974, Honduras had joined with other banana producers to form the Union of Banana Exporting Countries (UPEB).[16] The objective, following the example of oil-exporting nations that made up the Organization of Petroleum Exporting Countries (OPEC), was to secure better prices and to coordinate production and export policies. An export tax of one U.S. dollar per box was recommended in April 1974, but this was severely contested by the transnational banana companies. By the time the tax was implemented in August, a graduated scale had been devised that would result in twenty-five U.S. cents per box by 1979 (Decree Law No. 143, 23 August 1974). On 24 August, Minister of Economy Abraham Bennatón Ramos left for Europe, where he allegedly deposited $1.25 million in a Swiss bank account.

The struggle to revise relations between the banana companies and the state continued on into 1975. Cancellation of the historic concessions that had been granted to the banana producers were postponed twice—in November 1974 and in March 1975. The story about United Brands, bribe payments, and revised export taxes broke in mid-April 1975.[17] A week later, López Arellano was deposed as chief of state. His successor, Gen. Juan Melgar Castro, immediately created a presidential advisory committee on national banana policy. Its report of July 1975 recommended the government become involved in banana production, establish a state agency to oversee the nation's banana business, nationalize all docks and railroads, and finally move to acquire majority control of the foreign-owned companies.[18] In September, the UPEB agreement was ratified. The Honduran Banana Corporation (COHBANA) was created in October; in December, the National Port Enterprise (ENP) assumed control over the fruit-company docks at La Ceiba, Tela, and Puerto Cortés. In April 1976, the state acquired 306 kilometers of rail lines from the Tela Railroad Company and 450 kilometers from the Standard Fruit and Steamship Company. Agreements were made for the companies to keep and maintain the rolling stock for a period of eight years, after which the National Railroad of Honduras (FNH) would assume operational responsibility.

The sensational events of 1974–1975 occurred at a time when policymakers were seeking broad national reforms that would contribute toward Honduran national development. Domestic pressures to act against the large banana companies coincided with international efforts to help secure more control over the country's national resources.

For their part, the transnational banana companies had been raising productivity on land they still owned and diversifying into other fruit and vegetable export crops. Another trend was the shift toward local, associated banana producers. During the early 1950s, United Brands had begun to promote individual local producers, extending technical and other forms of assistance. From 1960 to 1977, the amount of lands devoted to banana cultivation by local producers increased from 19 to 35 percent of the national total. Similarly, the number of boxes produced by Honduran growers rose from a 1960–1962 average of 19 percent to 28 percent of national production in 1974–1977.[19]

This trend perhaps benefited the transnational companies more than either the state or the local producers. Both Tela Railroad and Standard Fruit were able to increase total production without rehabilitating older parcels or risking large investments in the development of new lands. Local producers and the state then assumed investment burdens and the inherent risks of weather, disease, and production. Thus, the companies, while maintaining what amounted to a monopoly on international marketing, were able to capture a lower political profile.

Worldwide recession and lowered prices helped to further reduce the operations of the fruit companies in Honduras and other countries in Central America. Standard Fruit announced in late 1982 that it would be moving all of its La Ceiba–based operations to Puerto Cortés. The immediate impact was a loss of more than seven hundred jobs in La Ceiba and the closing of docks, cargo railroad, and the D'Antoni Hospital. Critics and the Unified Syndicate of Standard Fruit Company Workers (SUTRASFCO) charged that the company was pressuring the government for lower export taxes.

Whether due to economic conditions, more immediate financial strategy, or the regional political crisis, the transnational companies have clearly established a pattern of reducing their economic and political risks in Honduras and elsewhere in Central America.

Development and Trade

Honduran development strategy as outlined in National Development Plans since 1974 assumes the acquisition of new technologies, necessary capital goods, and more infrastracture development—all requiring external resources in the form of direct imports or financing. This in turn necessitates continued investment in the country's productive sectors and enhancement of its export capacity. The Honduran economy performed better than expected during the latter part of the 1970s, averaging a 7.5 percent annual growth rate. This was due to a strong export market and a considerable rise in public-sector investment. By 1980, the economy had declined in the face of difficulties—coffee prices had dropped, energy costs had reached new highs, and a worldwide credit shortage coincided with an erosion of investor confidence in Central America.

The ability of Honduras to borrow rests upon the productivity of its export sector accompanied by constraints on its imports. Export income depends on the volume of production and the fluctuation of world commodity prices. The circle is closed when Honduran import requirements are considered in the context of development policies. The agribusiness sector relies upon certain goods, such as chemicals and equipment, that are imported. Most of the large development projects require imports of machinery, production systems, and a wide range of raw materials. As import costs rise, export income lags behind, leading to more external financing. This in turn increases the country's debt-service payment outflow. From 1973 to 1981, the ratio of debt-service payments more than tripled, rising from 3.7 percent to 12.7 percent of export income.[20]

Nearly 40 percent of the Honduran gross national product is derived from its foreign trade. Bananas have been the prime earner of foreign exchange since the 1900s when they provided more than half the income. During the 1930s and 1940s, the proportion provided by bananas rose to more than 80 percent. After 1950, even as banana exports increased in volume, the share of export income gradually declined to 27 percent in 1980. Even so, Honduras is still a major world producer, providing over 17 percent of the global supply in 1980.

The composition of Honduran exports has become more diversified since 1950, with coffee, meat, cotton, wood, and minerals adding to the nation's income (Figure 7.1). Manufactured products are relatively new to the export sector, but constituted 15 percent (by value) of exports in 1980. Regardless of the diversification, primary products still account for 70 percent of the export market; this proportion held steady throughout the 1960s and 1970s.

Most Honduran exports are destined for the United States, Europe, and Central American neighbors. Together, these markets constitute up to 85 percent of the country's foreign trade.[21] The U.S. share has dropped slightly since 1960, from an average 55 percent to 52 percent in 1980. In Europe, the leading trade partner is West Germany, followed by the Netherlands, Belgium, and Italy. Japan represents less than 4 percent of the global export market for Honduras. In the late 1960s, the Central American Common Market (CACM) represented an average 15 percent of export income. After the 1969 war with El Salvador, CACM was disrupted by the withdrawal of Honduras, and exports to CACM dropped to less than 3 percent.

The other side of the equation is the more diverse but ever-expanding import account. The United States, as Honduras's leading trade partner, supplies 42 percent; Europe's share varies from 12 to 16 percent; CACM's 12 percent is down from its high of 24 percent during the first years of the common market. Together, the United States, Europe, the CACM countries, and Japan originate about 80 percent of Honduran imports.

The revolution in energy costs and supply problems has severely impacted most developing economies. Honduras imports all of its crude petroleum, mostly from Venezuela, which accounted for 16 percent of all import costs in 1975. In 1980, the figure was 11 percent, but Mexico and Trinidad and Tobago accounted for another 6 percent. Besides fuels, leading imports are raw materials, machinery, transport equipment, chemical products, and foods along with diverse manufactured articles not available in Honduras. Continued economic growth and development are inevitably tied to energy supplies and other capital imports.

Assuming that import capacity can be sustained (manageable debt-service levels, sustained production of export goods), Honduras still must overcome serious obstacles to its overall economic and social development. The country's basic social development needs—such as education, health services, labor skills, and agricultural extension work—are immense. Various external factors further condition the success or failure of Honduran development efforts. To the structure of trade analyzed above are added the vagaries of world commodity prices, international financial markets, and regional politics. After 1978, the

Nicaraguan revolution and its impact within the region contributed to the exodus of private capital. The Honduran lempira has been maintained as a freely convertible currency for several decades. But as the regional conflict spread, Hondurans and other Central Americans (who converted their holdings into lempiras) began to transfer capital assets into dollar accounts, mainly in the United States or Europe. An estimated $1 billion of capital fled Honduras between 1979 and 1983. Export earnings were retained abroad and private foreign investors delayed or canceled plans to expand their operations in Honduras.

As both global and regional economic political dynamics became more complex, the obstacles to national development will also become more difficult to manage. Increased stress on the Honduran polity will have to be met with more effective delivery of essential services, economic planning, and the management of development projects. Demands for more land redistribution will have to be balanced against inexorable pressures to raise productivity in basic food crops in addition to expanding the nation's export capacity.

8

The Region and International Relations

Despite its historical isolation and belated integration with the global economy, the course of Honduran politics has been vitally linked to relations with the rest of Central America, the United States, and other countries of the Caribbean Basin. The United States has had a preponderant influence upon Honduran social and political development. Until the 1950s, U.S. influence was exercised through or on behalf of the mining or banana companies. It mattered little as to who headed the Honduran government as long as tax, concessionary, or other legal policies did not drastically alter the status of U.S. investments.

In the postwar environment of decolonization and chilling U.S.-Soviet relations, development assistance programs and defense of the free world became pillars of U.S. foreign policy. The Cuban revolution exacerbated competition between the United States and the Soviet Union as U.S. concepts of national security shifted from hemispheric defense to enhancing the counterinsurgency capabilities of local militaries. Economic integration and the formation of the Central American Common Market stimulated more diverse flows of foreign investment. International investment, financial and technical aid, and military training emerged as important factors in the shaping of Honduran institutions.

Honduran international relations and its foreign policy remain oriented toward and influenced by the United States. In recent years, however, because of growing trade relations and a desire to diversify its diplomatic contacts, Honduras has expanded its relations with Japan, Taiwan, and several nations in Western Europe. Its membership in the United Nations and the Organization of American States is also used to broaden international contacts. Diplomatic relations have yet to be established with the Soviet Union or Cuba, although relations with some Eastern European countries are maintained via embassies in other Central American countries.

Despite the successes of the Central American Common Market during the 1960s, Honduran relations with neighboring republics often have been uneasy whether because of unclarified border claims or allegations that Honduras has served as a launching pad for invasion. The 1969 war with El Salvador was the most dramatic example of this historical pattern in recent years.

Despite the country's attempt to avoid the worst of the regional conflicts, amid the explosions of revolutionary change in Nicaragua and El Salvador, the Central American crisis of the 1980s drew Honduras closer to center stage. U.S. regional interests were fervently rekindled. Other countries in Central America either courted Honduran support or feared the country's potential as a counterrevolutionary platform. Set within the context of Soviet-U.S. rivalry, Honduras and Central America had become a collection of political pawns.

CENTRAL AMERICAN COMMON MARKET

After World War II, the dream of Central American unity was revived in the guise of economic integration. The Economic Commission for Latin America (ECLA) encouraged nations of the region to restructure their economies, but it was recognized that economic development would be difficult without larger domestic markets. The Organization of Central American States (ODECA) was created in 1951; and after a series of preliminary agreements among Guatemala, El Salvador, Honduras, Nicaragua, and Costa Rica, the fundamental charter of the Central American Common Market (CACM) was signed in Managua.[1]

Through its first decade, CACM was deemed such a success that it surprised even those who supported economic integration. From 1961 to 1966, the region's gross domestic product averaged an annual 6.3 percent growth.[2] Foreign investment poured into CACM as barriers to Central American commerce were gradually reduced or eliminated. Industry grew and new businesses were created to take advantage of the larger consumer market. From 1960 to 1968, intraregional trade increased eight times, making up 25 percent of all Central American exports. But Honduran industrial expansion quickly slowed. Pressures began to build as Honduras, Nicaragua, and Costa Rica experienced negative import-export balances with Guatemala and El Salvador. While Honduras exported its agricultural products to Central America, much of the extraregional investment was attracted to already existing infrastructures in El Salvador and Guatemala, and Honduran industry had difficulty competing with more efficiently manufactured goods from Guatemala, El Salvador, and in some cases Costa Rica. Under these conditions, opposition to continued participation in the common market arose within Honduras.

CACM had come to the end of easy economic expansion, and basic structural and production problems could be avoided no longer.

Dissatisfaction on the part of Honduras was evident. But Costa Rica was also threatening to take unilateral measures in order to correct its own trade imbalances. With the 1969 conflict between El Salvador and Honduras, the situation was exacerbated as the latter closed its doors to Salvadoran trade and commerce.

In 1970, the Central American economic ministers met in Managua to devise a *modus operandi* for maintaining integration on a temporary basis while efforts were made to revise the bases of the common market. The agreement proposed an industrial fund designed to help resolve Honduran and Nicaraguan complaints about unequal participation in Central American trade. These negotiations stumbled over the acrimony that remained between El Salvador and Honduras. Meanwhile, Honduras declared its withdrawal from CACM. At the same time, the president of Honduras was authorized to undertake bilateral negotiations to establish reciprocal trade relations with its former common market partners. Commercial treaties were contracted with Guatemala, Nicaragua, and Costa Rica; trade patterns, with some adjustments, resumed close to normal proportions even though Honduras and El Salvador traded with just three other countries.

Any prospect for reconstructing CACM had to first resolve the outstanding differences between Honduras and El Salvador. The way was cleared in October 1980 when a treaty was finally signed (see the next section). In addition, the original CACM treaty expired in June 1981. Though the opportunity was present, the path toward rejuvenating the common market has not been easy to resume. Regional political differences have become much more salient than those of three decades before. Domestic violence racks El Salvador and Guatemala, and the "seedlings of oppression" have broken the surface in Honduras.

Another factor affecting the prospects of normalized common market relations is the disarray in world economies. Decline in economic growth, high interest rates, and global inflation have a multiplied effect on Central American economies. The import of technology, capital goods, and loans has become more costly. The result is still more pressure on balance-of-payment deficits as world market conditions deteriorate for the traditional exports of Honduras. At the same time, given the political crises of the region, investment conditions in Central America have not been favorable.

Any revival of CACM must overcome shifting national differences and domestic opposition to altering status quo conditions that have been tortuously arrived at since 1969. Regardless, rather than transient economic problems, it is the basic structural difficulties of the Central American economies—dependence on the export of primary products, declining terms of trade, rising external debts—that influence the future of the common market. Also absent is any external catalyst such as the United States or UN agencies—a role they played during the 1950s—that might stimulate some resolve to deal with the core issues. As regional interests are diverging, there is only minimal outside sponsorship of Central American integration. Under these conditions, the future of economic integration does not seem very promising until political discord within Central America has moderated.

CENTRAL AMERICAN RELATIONS

Another dimension of intraregional relations has been represented by the Central American Defense Council (CONDECA), formally established in 1964.[3] The concept of regional defense was first proposed in the Declaration of Antigua (1955), and an outline of CONDECA was devised by the so-called Managua Commission in 1961. The idea was supported originally by Guatemala, Nicaragua, and Honduras; later, it was accepted by El Salvador and Costa Rica. CONDECA was to coordinate military strategy on matters pertinent to regional defense, enhance collective defense capabilities, and promote standardized command structures, training procedures, and equipment.

CONDECA reflected a distinct shift in U.S. thinking about its own security interests in the Caribbean Basin. From 1942 to 1960, global confrontation with the Soviet Union dominated defense policy. The United States and Latin America were formally obligated to cooperate on defense of the Western Hemisphere against external aggression under terms of the 1947 Rio Treaty. But the Cuban revolution and signs of unrest in other countries in the region caused a revision of U.S. security policy after 1961. The dangers of internal subversion and domestic political instability became the focus of defense policy and national-security doctrine. It was in this light that Central America was declared a geographic unity and countries of that area were encouraged to set up a regional defense council. CONDECA coincided with the Alliance for Progress, which included civic-action programs for Latin American militaries. However, revised security doctrines and expanded internal roles tended to reinforce the autonomy of Central American militaries within their respective national political systems. Since the armed forces were the major power contenders in Honduras, El Salvador, Guatemala, and Nicaragua, this autonomy was sometimes achieved at the expense of the old and new civilian political sectors.

CONDECA functioned on a regional basis only informally, punctuated by infrequent joint military exercises and other collaborative aspects. For the most part, contact within Central America was based on personal relationships among military officers and communications facilitated by the United States. In broad terms, CONDECA was seen to serve U.S. interests more so than those of the countries in Central America. On the other hand, the embattled traditional elites have defended its necessity and role in the region.

Any initial unity or cooperation that had been established was undermined by early stresses in the Central American Common Market and the shock of the 1969 border conflict between Honduras and El Salvador. After the war, Honduras changed its status within CONDECA to that of an observer. During the 1970s, Anastasio Somoza D. was highly agitated over the "reformist" government of López Arellano because its policies set "bad" examples for the stability of Nicaragua and other countries in Central America. The Sandinista campaigns of 1978 and 1979 added to the divisions, and intervention by extraregional powers helped to further polarize Central America.

Relations within the region during the early 1980s made any revival of CONDECA an unlikely possibility. El Salvador's urgent call to revive military cooperation was supported by Guatemala, but Gen. Policarpo Paz García, the provisional president of Honduras, elected to retain his country's public stance of neutrality. However, in January 1983, the Honduran government expressed an interest in the revival of the regional defense pact. The idea was said to be under study by the Honduran military command, and it was thought the idea might be presented to all of the Central American countries including Nicaragua and Panama.

THE 1969 WAR WITH EL SALVADOR

The positive dynamics of regional economic integration had generated their own contradictions as the Honduran economy suffered excessive trade deficits. Intraregional stress reached a high point in 1969 when El Salvador's army invaded the southern and western portions of Honduras. Open conflict between the two countries lasted only four days, but more than three thousand people were killed in what international media quickly dubbed the "soccer war."[4]

Causes of the short-lived war had been building over time. Though the spark that set off the four-day war was a series of incidents surrounding soccer matches between Honduran and Salvadoran teams, the underlying causes were long-developing demographic trends. Over the years, population pressures in El Salvador had prodded its citizens to migrate to Honduras. Land was relatively more available in Honduras, and job opportunities attracted laborers to the enclave economy on the North Coast. While peasants sowed and harvested on idle lands, enterprising Salvadorans were also involved in the agribusiness economy, cultivating cotton and other cash crops. The dispute arose when increasingly organized and effective peasant organizations pressured the government to actively enforce provisions of the 1962 Agrarian Reform Law. An easy target was the aliens who occupied or worked lands, especially those Salvadorans who were competing directly with Hondurans. Squatters and others were evicted, sometimes with force, causing a reversal in the migratory flow from El Salvador. Furthermore, an ill-defined boundary and the overall imbalance of common market benefits had complicated Honduran relations with El Salvador. The outstanding bilateral issues, though critical, were not unresolvable or so serious as to lead inevitably to war. Rather, it was the impact of these issues on each country's politics and the response of domestic political elites to subsequent pressures that eventually forced open hostilities.

A migration treaty was not renewed when it expired in January 1969. The two-year agreement had regulated the status of an estimated 300,000 alien Salvadorans and established procedures to deal with future immigration to Honduras. President López Arellano and his government had instead other problems in trying to resolve conflicting internal demands. The rural peasant movement had stepped up its campaign for more land distribution, and labor unions supported efforts to limit the employment of aliens in agribusiness industries. But with land utilization turning more toward cash-crop production, commercial ranchers and farmers welcomed the supply of laborers who willingly accepted lower wages.

Persistent trade problems within the Central American Common Market had reduced Honduran revenues from imports and exports. Although trade among the five member countries had been liberalized for manufactured goods, it had not been for agricultural products. The impact, or costs, of economic integration thus was felt more keenly in the "developed" enclave along the North Coast of Honduras. Attempts to compensate for lost revenue through taxes on income, profits, and capital assets were resisted by the newer socioeconomic elites.

Discontent over economic stagnation and ineffectual governmental performance gained momentum as business, labor, and peasant leaders aggressively lobbied for administrative reforms, liberal public-sector investment, and a variety of social measures that would benefit the working class and rural poor. The occupation of lands by organized peasant groups, and the outrage of stock raisers and large landholders eventually required some type of response from the government.

The 1968-1969 crisis between landless peasants and landholders had reached near epidemic proportions. Regulations of the 1962 Agrarian Reform Law provided that only natural-born citizens were eligible to receive lands distributed by the National Agrarian Institute (INA). After being ignored for several years, political conditions now favored strict enforcement of citizenship requirements. Lands were made available by evicting Salvadoran subsistence farmers who had been in Honduras up to ten or more years but had failed to regularize their status as alien residents. The law was applied in a discriminatory manner, an action that enabled the Honduran government to avoid a confrontation with adamant Honduran landowners, since few if any private holdings were affected during this period.

The widespread evictions and a growing anti-Salvadoran mood induced a mass exodus of people back to their homeland. This reversal of normal migration patterns caused anxiety among political leaders in El Salvador. The long-term relief valve of emigration to Honduras had been closed, exacerbating tensions in El Salvador that were already barely contained. El Salvador broke diplomatic relations on 27 June 1969. Three weeks later, on 14 July, the attack was made into Honduras. El Salvador's ultimate objective was to quickly capture territory and utilize its possession as a bargaining tool. Such plans were negated by the unexpected resistance of the Honduran armed forces. Though not as prepared militarily, the Honduran army was able to hold its own, backed up by the surprising effectiveness of its air force. Perhaps more important, the four-day war also galvanized Honduran citizens, especially the rural sectors, in defense of the national territory. With military action stagnated, an offer by the Organization of American States (OAS) to mediate presented El Salvador the opportunity to withdraw its forces with some dignity.

The sense of nationalism on the part of Honduras, which rescued the regime from the more immediate political pressures, had more profound impacts on domestic political developments. For one, the Honduran military was forced to reexamine its overall defensive strategy and personnel requirements. Second, the leadership, including President López Arellano, had come face to face with the conditions of poverty that afflicted most Hondurans. And third, these events stimulated some consensus within the Honduran armed forces about the need for social and economic reforms. Importantly, the heroic defense of the country dissipated much of the ill will that had followed the repressive 1963 military coup. The Honduran armed forces now symbolized the nation's pride and elevated self-confidence.

The 1969 war brought regional strains to the surface. Severed diplomatic relations were accompanied by closure of the border with El Salvador. Honduras denied passage to all vehicles except those registered in a third country. This severely affected the common market's commerce and transportation network by splitting the region in half. The position of Honduras was stubbornly maintained for more than a decade. Negotiations were strained at first, but under OAS auspices a series of mediation efforts were conducted in different capitals.

Both countries were able to live with the status quo for more than ten years. But with the Nicaraguan revolution and acceleration of violence in El Salvador, conditions then facilitated a rapid end to more than four years of negotiations. On 30 October 1980, a treaty ending hostilities between El Salvador and Honduras was signed; ten days later, the National Constituent Assembly (ANC) ratified the agreement. The treaty also committed both countries to revitalization of the Central American Common Market, but set no timetable. Meanwhile, a bilateral agreement concluded in March 1981 regulated the reestablishment of trade relations. Strangely enough the long-lived border issue was finessed, giving that responsibility to a binational border commission over a five-year period. The effective "militarization" of the disputed pockets of territory (*bolsones*) along the border was accomplished, as all prohibitions about military operations in those zones were now lifted. This portion of the treaty also accommodated the interests of the "hard-line" military leaders in Honduras as well as important aspects of U.S. policy toward Central America. The *bolsones* had become sanctuaries for Salvadoran guerilla forces, and both militaries were anxious to eradicate these zones. Honduras wished to avoid spillover of the Salvadoran civil war, and the United States was hoping to contain the violence and contagion of revolutionary change.

THE HONDURAN ROLE IN CENTRAL AMERICA

The Central American crisis began to unfold in 1978, and then broke open in 1979 with the Sandinista defeat of the Somoza regime. The reaction of other Central American republics helped to define an initial polarization of relations within the region. Both Panama and Costa Rica had been involved in support of the Sandinista Front prior to Somoza's exit from power. Meanwhile, the northern tier countries— Guatemala, El Salvador, and Honduras—looked upon the disintegration of the government in Nicaragua and pondered what implications the revolution might have for their own political systems. Somoza's links with Guatemala and El Salvador had been especially close. The military governors in Honduras preferred stability, but their major concern was to avoid embroiling themselves in Nicaragua's civil war.

The early pattern of polarization in Central America became less distinct as the Sandinista government became more authoritarian.[5] Relations between Panama and Nicaragua quickly cooled when Cuban assistance and advisers supplanted offers of help from Gen. Omar Torrijos. Meanwhile, domestic political and economic problems distracted Costa Rica's leadership, who feared any prospect of political violence in their country. Somoza had been regarded as a threat to Costa Rican stability, but as Nicaragua's leaders sought to consolidate their hold on power, an element of disillusionment about the revolution spread within Costa Rica.

The northern pole of countries fused its ranks in opposition to the Sandinista government, especially when the violence in El Salvador flared up in mid-1979. When the United States finally turned its attention toward Central America, it found a situation that was slightly out of control. The forces of political change had been gathering for at least a decade or more. And amid the patterns of changing global power relations, other nations in the Caribbean Basin had established their influence within Central America.

With the beginning of the 1980s, the Republic of Honduras suddenly assumed a new geopolitical status. Its key location in the middle of the Central American isthmus separated Nicaragua from Guatemala, El Salvador, and Mexico. Despite being ruled by military governments for over a decade, Honduran society and politics did not yet exhibit the overt violence that afflicted its closest neighbors to the north. This image of calm was augmented by progress toward the return of constitutional government. Elections in 1980 had been enthusiastically supported by a heavy voter response, and preparations were in full swing for the selection of a civilian administration at the end of 1981. This apparent tranquility made Honduras a logical choice to represent the Central American alternative to revolutionary change. Regional events and global competition had conspired to make Honduras an arena for external involvement for the next decade or longer.

HONDURAS AND ITS NEIGHBORS

The geostrategic importance of Honduras in Central America had already been demonstrated during the 1969 border war and the disruption of the common market. During the 1980s, an abrupt change of regime in Nicaragua and the revolutionary drama in El Salvador inserted a heightened sense of urgency into the region. It followed that Honduras's relations with its neighbors were transformed into issues critically important not only to the future course of regional events but also to the evolution of domestic politics.

Honduras has been the destination of thousands of refugees since 1978. Escaping the violence of battle or fearing physical retribution from paramilitary or government forces, almost forty thousand people had fled into the country by 1981.[6] Nicaraguan refugees were a mixture of classes fleeing the bombardment of cities and towns by Somoza's air force. Many who left after the Sandinista victory were identified as *somocistas*, or remnants of the infamous national guard. Another sizable element of refugees has been those who have entered Honduras from Zelaya province in northeastern Nicaragua. Mainly Indians, nearly fifteen thousand have settled in Gracias a Dios since 1981. Finally, a small but steady stream of Nicaraguans who have grown disillusioned with the Sandinista government continues to flow into Honduras. Besides posing an economic and social problem (in terms of job competition, unemployment, crime, and relief aid), the presence of perhaps five thousand ex-guardsmen has created international frictions. The issue between Nicaragua and Honduras has been to what extent these exiles, or *contras*, are involved with the incursions into Nicaraguan territory and whether or not Honduran authorities condoned or even fomented these activities. The government of Honduras periodically and emphatically has denied both the existence and official support of any such counterrevolutionary groups, blaming border raids on irresponsible and criminal elements.

Throughout 1981 and 1982, confrontations between Honduran and Sandinista military patrols escalated in number and intensity. Artillery fire was exchanged near the southern town of Guasaule, 44 kilometers from the city of Choluteca. Rumors of an impending invasion by Honduras have been a constant theme of Nicaragua's foreign-policy statements. A military spokesman added to the confusion by stating that "war with

Nicaragua was inevitable." Hard-line factions within the Honduran military command may have favored at least the probability of war in order to stymie the 1981 elections and reemphasize the national dominance of the armed forces. Questions were raised as to whether Honduras might be supporting territorial incursions in order to "destabilize" the Sandinista government or whether U.S. military aid had found its way into the hands of the *contra* forces.[7] By 1982, it had become apparent that the renegades were being financed by monies arriving from Guatemala City and Miami. Argentine advisers were working with the Honduran military and, under the guise of "businessmen," were involved in the anti-Sandinista movement. An unofficial radio station, the 15th of September—located on private property just outside of Tegucigalpa—had been in operation for some time programming anti-Sandinista broadcasts and propagandizing the exiles' return to Nicaragua.

Between official and unofficial denials of counterdenials, a serious outbreak of hostilities nearly occurred in August and September 1982. Meanwhile, both governments had attempted to maintain communications at both high and low diplomatic levels. The provisional president, Policarpo Paz García, had met with Sandinista leader Daniel Ortega in May 1981 to diffuse tensions. Subsequent meetings between Sandinista military leaders and Honduran battalion commanders have served to keep the channels open. Though more professional than in 1969, the Honduran armed forces—facing two troublesome borders—are outnumbered by Nicaraguan units.[8] Moreover, Mexico has reiterated its diplomatic support of Nicaragua; there is doubt about how much popular support Hondurans would lend to any war effort.

Relations with Nicaragua have gone through several phases since 1979, most characterized by mutual suspicion and growing animosity. In contrast, official relations with El Salvador improved dramatically during the same period. Coordination between respective military commands attained a significant degree of formality with the reestablishment of diplomatic relations following the 1980 peace treaty. The intent of Honduran leaders was to avoid any domestic upheavals that might be stimulated from El Salvador. A complicating aspect was the massive exodus of peasants and villagers from the Salvadoran provinces of Chalatenango, Cabañas, and Morazán. Honduran authorities viewed the refugees less favorably than those from Nicaragua, associating them with the insurgent forces. Efforts of international agencies and other groups to alleviate refugee conditions have encountered diffident attitudes and suspicion on the part of Honduran officials.

This position conformed with the predilection of most military commanders, who were concerned about national security and the possible "contamination" of revolutionary activity from El Salvador. Similar concerns also preoccupied U.S. policymakers. The momentum tended to strengthen Honduran-Salvadoran relations. New problems intervened as news accounts filtered out about mass killings along the mountainous frontier. Military operations in El Salvador against guerrilla strongholds left few options for provincial residents except to flee their homes. Meanwhile, units of the Honduran Twelfth Battalion had been trying to stem the tide of refugees.

The function or role of the Honduran armed forces in the Salvadoran operations has never been adequately clarified. In October 1981 the general staffs of both militaries conferred in the border town of El Amatillo. During 1982, coordination between Salvadoran and Honduran security forces expanded. In June, Honduran units conducted a sweep along the frontier occupying several of the bolsones. Gen. Gustavo Alvarez Martínez, head of the armed forces, indicated that the Salvadoran and Guatemalan armies were collaborating in the exchange of information as well as providing support to each other in certain military operations.[9] By 1983, with U.S. assistance and support, Honduras had been successful in stemming the flow of arms from Nicaragua into El Salvador by land and sea, although shipments were still being carried out in a variety of light aircraft. To monitor the latter channel of arms traffic, U.S. plans were announced in early 1983 to establish a radar station in southeastern Honduras.

In the midst of growing tensions, Honduran foreign policy developed in several directions. In part this was a reflection of the complex situation the country found itself in, but also it was due to differing perceptions and goals within the policymaking circles. Any direct conflict with Nicaragua or worsening of El Salvador's internal violence would threaten the country. The Honduran army was not prepared for any sustained operation against Sandinista security forces; in addition, any military conflict on such a scale would have invited further ruin upon an already shaky economy. Nevertheless, as evidence of anti-Sandinista activity mounted, and as the insurgent forces in El Salvador began to be affected by Honduran efforts to control the porous frontier, the country became a focal point for externally supported subversion and terror. Bombings, airline hijackings, destruction of the Tegucigalpa electrical system, and the September 1982 hostage drama in San Pedro Sula were designed to warn Hondurans, to create internal divisions, and polarize the relationship between authorities and the population. "Internationalizing" the conflict in part served to distract both Honduran and U.S. policy strategists, and it also may have alleviated pressures upon insurgent forces in El Salvador. At the same time, Nicaragua's leaders accused Honduras (and the United States) of preparing for a massive invasion into their country. Among the "hard-liners" in the Honduran military, the idea of striking out against Nicaragua did acquire some momentum, although there was some doubt as to how far the United States would support that course of action. But with the mid-1982 publicity about "covert" operations, contras operating out of Honduras, and the "secret war" against Nicaragua, the bellicose posturing quickly subsided.

In contrast to the confrontational trend, President Suazo Córdova, Foreign Minister Eduardo Paz Barnica, and others among the so-called peace faction attempted to "internationalize" the peace. Key to this policy was the perception that Honduran security and national interests would be served best through a regional approach. In January 1982, prior to Suazo's assumption of the presidency, the foreign ministers of Costa Rica, El Salvador, and Honduras established the Central American Democratic Community (CDC). Its aims were to create a climate of security in the region, promote democratic values, and enhance the opportunity for economic development. The agreement also affirmed the goals of mutual solidarity, particularly in those situations where members of the CDC might be targets of aggression or international pressure.

The CDC was attacked by Nicaragua as "anti-democratic," and both Panama and Guatemala complained at not being invited to join. The fledgling pact, however, was endorsed by Venezuela, Colombia, and the United States. Moreover, the three countries were to become observer nations of the CDC. Guatemala was included as a member soon after Efraín Ríos Montt emerged as chief of state.

The official position of the Honduran government was that the country was positively neutral in the regional conflict. It was stated repeatedly that an armed invasion of Nicaragua was neither desired nor contemplated. Foreign Minister Paz Barnica insisted that anti-Sandinista camps did not exist; but General Alvarez admitted during press interviews that along the isolated Honduran-Nicaraguan border there probably were bands of anti-Sandinistas. He added that he felt no great responsibility or urgency to control such groups while Nicaragua used Honduran territory to transport arms and support Honduran terrorists.

Regardless, a broad effort was made to involve democratic Caribbean nations in the Honduran campaign for peace. The foreign minister presented a six-point peace plan for Central America at the March 1982 meeting of the Organization of American States. The proposal advocated (1) a general disarmament in the region, (2) the reduction of foreign military and other advisers, (3) multilateral observation and supervision of sensitive areas, (4) means to cease arms traffic in the region, (5) respect for delimited and demarcated borders and traditional lines of jurisdiction, and (6) establishment of a permanent multilateral dialogue that would eventually strengthen democratic and pluralistic institutions and practices in Central America.

Six months later, the Mexican and Venezuelan presidents, José López Portillo and Luis Herrera Campíns, sent President Suazo Córdova as well as the leaders of Nicaragua and the United States a letter expressing their concern over the spreading violence. In particular, they offered to help mediate the impending conflict between Honduras and Nicaragua. The Mexican-Venezuelan diplomatic initiative was essentially ignored by both Honduras and the United States.[10]

Instead, encouraged by the United States, Honduras joined Belize, Colombia, El Salvador, Jamaica, and the Dominican Republic on 4 October to organize the Forum for Peace and Democracy in San José,

Costa Rica. The six points of the Honduran regional peace proposal were included as part of the final act.[11] More attempts were made to encourage Mexico, Venezuela, and other Caribbean nations to support the goals of the Forum.

Honduras, most likely with support from the United States, was attempting to mobilize regional involvement in some overall resolution of the Central American crisis. One objective for Honduras was to gather a "democratic" majority that might be able to isolate or pressure Nicaragua into a more flexible and less aggressive stance. On the other hand, given the centrality of Honduras in the region's geopolitics, many leaders feared a clash with either Nicaragua or insurgent forces from within. Left alone, the prospects for Honduras did not seem overly optimistic, thus, the constant attempts to involve Mexico, Venezuela, and other Caribbean nations in the Forum and other proposed multilateral diplomatic initiatives that might have diffused regional tensions.

NEW RELATIONS IN THE CARIBBEAN BASIN

Very early in 1983, the foreign ministers of Mexico, Venezuela, and Colombia met in Panama to discuss Central America and assess the several peace initiatives that had been tendered by different countries. Although other nations could help, it was emphasized that only the countries directly involved in any potential conflict would ultimately reach satisfactory solutions, and that none could be imposed. Mexico and Venezuela affirmed their continued "energy" support as outlined in the oil-facility agreement. They had agreed in 1980 to guarantee petroleum supplies to Central America and other countries in the Caribbean Basin.[12] The cooperative energy plan provided that 30 percent of oil-import costs could be deferred over a five-year period at 4 percent interest. However, if the monies released under these provisions were invested in national development schemes, the recipient country would enjoy more liberal repayment of twenty years at 2 percent interest. The oil facility was intended to relieve balance-of-payment pressures on importing nations and assist them in transferring scarce resources into economic development programs.

In July 1981, Mexico and Venezuela met with the United States and Canada to discuss multilateral economic assistance to nations in the Caribbean Basin. Political and philosophical differences were evident, but the consensus was that aid was sorely needed by most developing countries in the region. Despite its difficulties, the U.S. Caribbean Basin Initiative did provide $350 million in loans and grants to several countries. Only $35 million went to Honduras. These amounts were easily surpassed by the sacrifice that Venezuela and Mexico have made through their oil subsidy.

Perhaps more important for Honduras and other Central American republics is merely the fact that Mexico, Venezuela, Colombia, and other nations have demonstrated their interests in the region. Both the oil-exporting nations have exercised wider influence throughout the Caribbean Basin and have become more involved in Central American affairs since 1975. This phenomenon is a product of increased Third World awareness and the new capacity of some developing countries to resist or even challenge major-power domination. The other side of the coin is, however, the possibility of expanding Cuban and Soviet influence in Central America. Certainly, this potential is viewed by most countries of the region with no small amount of trepidation, and it has been an integral aspect of the revolutionary pressures present in most of the Central American societies.

Challenges to U.S. dominance over Central America and within the Caribbean by emerging regional powers has broadened Honduran foreign-policy options. Ties with the United States will remain substantial, but a historical turn has been made with more diverse international contacts. Taiwan, Korea, Israel, and Argentina have become additional sources for military assistance, arms, and training. Mexico, Venezuela, Japan, and Europe have evolved as important trading partners, and all have offered valuable bilateral economic assistance and investment possibilities. From the perception of Honduras, the new regional powers could possibly serve as a counterbalance to Cuban interference and modify to some extent U.S. hegemony.

THE CENTRAL AMERICAN CRISIS
AND HONDURAN DEVELOPMENT

New relations in the Caribbean Basin once again raise the question of Honduras's geopolitical importance, and the struggle being waged in Central America harbors direct consequences for the country's political evolution. Regional conflict has already disrupted the country's economic trade and commercial relations; political discord has sown nervousness among both civilian and military elites.

Any assumptions about the political evolution of Honduras must consider the susceptibility of the polity to external influences. The dynamics of Central American geopolitics are likely to continue in the historical pattern in which Honduran territory is used as a transit zone or as a base for counterrevolutionary movements. Conversely, Honduras is also likely to become the target of revolutionary forces. The problem is how to evaluate and distinguish Honduran national interests versus those thrust upon the country by U.S. strategic interests or those of other Caribbean powers. Any major counterrevolutionary role for Honduras will increase pressures upon the government. Full-scale conflict (e.g., an invasion of Nicaragua) would further destroy relations in Central America and the flow of refugees would impact most on Honduras.

Although there are serious reservations about the extent of support among Hondurans for such an aggressive foreign policy, there is also doubt whether counterrevolutionary action would generate a full-scale leftist revolt in Honduras, particularly in the face of any direct U.S. support. To carry the scenario further, direct intervention on the part of the United States would present long-term consequences for Honduran political development. International attention and revolutionary forces would gravitate toward Honduras and Central America with even more intensity, thus raising the specter of Soviet-U.S. confrontation in the region. Direct intervention could polarize the society, irreversibly, condemning the traditional political elite to a certain demise. Any prospect of socioeconomic reform that might be carried out by centrist (bourgeois) political sectors would likely be lost.[13] On balance, the course of events in Central America and the wider context of international pressures detract from the attention that needs to be directed toward national development, socioeconomic reform, and steps that might be taken to integrate the mass of Honduran citizens into the society and its political process.

9

The Politics
of Frustration

The transition from *caudillismo* to rule by military governors occupied Honduras for more than thirty years. The seeds of change planted during the 1920s and 1930s within the enclave economy were revived with international ties that developed rapidly after World War II. Diversity in the export market impacted on rural, precapitalistic Honduras as land-use patterns and traditional relations shifted in favor of landed elites and agribusiness enterprise. During the same period, social differentiation and economic diversity helped to disperse power and stimulated the realignment of old elites and new sociopolitical forces. Since 1950, as we have seen, one major development has been the growth of the state and a central government apparatus and its assumption of more social and economic functions. Second, demands for increased political participation came from new sociopolitical sectors—urban middle classes, the burgeoning labor movement, rural peasant groups, and a complex array of private enterprise organizations. A third aspect was the emergence of a nationally organized, professional military institution. Finally, the traditional political elites, coalesced around the Liberal and National political parties, began to lose viability as they failed to grasp the significance and impact of rapid, fundamental social and economic change in Honduras.

The halting, inconclusive process of adjusting to these modernizing conditions has concerned Honduran political elites whether traditional, progressive, popular, or military in nature. The old forms of personalistic politics and authoritarian rule by themselves were not adequate to cope with demands originating from the newer social and political sectors. Political uncertainty in the years following the retirement of General Carías was checked by military coups, fluctuating civil-military alliances, and—after the mid-1970s—military domination over the state.

Honduran national integration never has had a strong history. In the environment of social ferment after World War II, the emergence

121

of new social classes, proliferation of organized groups, loosening of traditional relations, and crystallization of new channels of communication—both horizontal and vertical—outside the historical political parties added new dimensions of fragmentation to the already tenuous historical base. The dispersal of power among old and new groups complicated the task of responding to the pressures of modernization. As a result, reforms that were implemented were left incomplete. As political realignments occurred, government policies and actions wavered between encouraging wider political participation and repressing or curtailing participation in the political process.

Against this background, the pattern that evolved was a cycle of frustration wherein social and political tensions would build, then be released under the guise of elections, a military coup, or hastily conceived stopgap policies. With each revolution of the cycle, the reduction of tensions has become more difficult to achieve.

FRAGMENTATION OF THE POLITY

Social isolation, geographic isolation, and other barriers to national political unity affected the nature of Honduran politics even until the late 1950s. During the era of Liberal reforms, effective national authority was frustrated by considerable difficulties in communication among regions, continuing rivalry among local political bosses, and finite resources available to the state. Besides the state, there were few if any early institutions that might have served as focal points for national identity. The colonial government of Spain was preoccupied with other, more lucrative parts of its realm. Honduras was on the edge of the Spanish empire—a pattern that echoed the reach of Mayan culture into the northwestern mountains. Religious issues were underplayed during the Liberal-Conservative struggles of the nineteenth century. The Honduran Catholic church, poor to begin with, was left weakened and in no position to serve as a node of national orientation. There was no formally organized armed force. Instead, "generals" and later the traditional political parties gathered bands of armed supporters to defend political gains or intimidate the opposition.

Traditional social relations based on personal ties emphasized localism, which was reinforced by the subsistence quality of small-farm production levels and the low productivity of the landed estates. There was little reason to produce surplus crops since there was little contact with world market forces. The establishment of an enclave society along the North Coast in the late nineteenth century by foreign investors precipitated a division of the Honduran economic structure between traditional agriculture and a commercial-agribusiness, externally oriented sector. Migration to the North Coast region was stimulated, but the enclave economy fulfilled most of its needs through imports.

The combination of physical isolation, absence of viable national institutions, and freewheeling values of personal gain produced regionalism, strong-man rule, and the instability of caudillo politics. The Honduran polity was fragmented as power was dispersed among regionally based factions, and economic influence represented by foreign investors in mining and export agriculture displaced any immediate prospects of Hondurans gaining control over their national resources.

For those without large expanses of land, economic opportunities were restricted. As the nineteenth-century state promoted its policies of Liberal reform, the interests of Honduran elites became associated more and more with foreign-owned enterprises. With government serving as an intermediary, capturing political control over the state then became the focal point for political competition and struggle. Electoral manipulations, armed rebellion, and civil wars were justified in the all-consuming desire to capture power. Once in a position of public authority, personal benefits could be assured.

Tiburcio Carías Andino represented the first significant departure from the established pattern of political instability. The Carías regime introduced political discipline, fiscal conservatism, and the stability of imposed authoritarian rule. The perennial cycle of rebellion was ended with the caudillo's iron grip upon the machinery of government and a personalistic despotism practiced within the National party. Carías brought about a semblance of national unity as authority was gradually centralized, and challenges from dissident "generals" provoked political exile, jail, and occasionally death. This stability, however, did not evolve organically as part of a growing national consensus, but rather was forced upon the political system. Highly personalistic, the Carías government lacked a body of principles and practices that might have served the polity once the period had come to an end. In this sense, the national unity that was accomplished was somewhat artificial.

The overlay of political peace was peeled away after World War II. Carías, pressured by the United States and with waning support of the United Fruit Company, reluctantly gave his blessing to Juan Manuel Gálvez as his successor. Postwar international contacts by governmental and private institutions shattered Honduran isolation. Demands for cotton, meat, coffee, and other primary commodities created new economic conditions and affected land-use patterns in Honduras.

To some extent, better communication networks and infrastructure development overcame divisions and established better links among the regions. Rural social relations were eroded, and the beginnings of class awareness surfaced as people began to have experiences beyond their local communities. At the same time, rural-oriented programs of the Catholic church and the organizing efforts of the labor movement helped create conditions favorable to the emergence of a grass-roots peasant movement. Deteriorating relationships, economic change, and overall population growth heightened the pace of internal migration and hastened urban expansion. New economic and social groups appeared as a direct result of new international contacts. The middle classes expanded along with growing opportunities for education and employment in the industrial-commercial sectors. Rising social and political awareness and development programs countered some of the geographical and socio-economic aspects of national fragmentation, but these same forces also precipitated divisions among traditional ruling groups as newer elites challenged their monopoly of political control.

Honduran society had entered into a fluid stage in which there was no coherent focus among the ruling groups. Besides the political competition offered by the new social strata, the traditional classes were faced with development problems that had been neglected for too long. The polity vibrated as governments were inundated by demands for social and economic reform and the prospect of integrating new socio-political groups into the political process.

CAUDILLOS AND COLONELS

Under the liberalized policies of the Gálvez government, numerous political challenges to the status quo appeared. The control of Carías over the National party inevitably relaxed, and internal discipline eased. The weakness of the retired dictator's political legacy was exposed as the Nationalists split into factions. Personalistic government and loyalty to the caudillo had left little room for new political leaders to gain experience and national exposure. As a result, the National party, with the possible exception of Gálvez himself, could offer no visionary leadership. The Liberal party was in no better shape, but for different reasons. The organization and ranks of the PLH had suffered from exile of its leadership and the more than two decades out of power. Disorganized, the Liberals were finally able to rally around Rámon Villeda Morales, but factions still plagued the party.

The traditional elites of Honduras were unable to resolve internecine squabbles as chaos reminiscent of the old caudillo struggles reappeared. There was no realistic perspective on the nature of the socioeconomic change that was transforming Honduras. Nor was there any evaluation of political implications beyond protecting the status quo. The Liberal government from 1957 to 1963 did, however, signal its intentions of instituting social and economic reforms, and the administration headed by Villeda Morales was able to accommodate the more urgent demands of organized labor, urban middle classes, and ambitious industrial-agribusiness entrepreneurs. Even so, the essence of caudillo politics endured, as the threat of rebellion against Villeda Morales never really subsided.

The framework of traditional politics had been disrupted by pressures of social and economic change, but modernization had also produced new social strata. The advent of the labor movement after 1954 was a major turning point for Honduran political development. The ultimate challenge to outmoded political values and the traditional power structure was to come from a rising political consciousness and the organization of nontraditional political sectors. Insofar as the historical political parties failed to integrate these emergent sociopolitical sectors, direct channels of political communication between progressive and popular-sector organizations and the state were formed outside the Liberal and National party networks. Given the record of abortive and fraudulent elections and the apparent inability or unwillingness of the political parties to broaden their political bases, it was only logical for the new sectors to seek alternative means of contact with an expanding state. Importantly, the resources offered by the state (and other organizations)—financial and technical assistance, investment incentives, land distribution, and legal recognition—were more attractive to the new participants than the empty promises and exclusionary attitudes of the traditional party leadership.

The sociopolitical forces of organized labor, an active peasant movement, and North Coast business groups, however, were not adequately formed to govern without a major shift in the political balance of power. The urban-rural division, though reduced, remained a key characteristic of Honduran society. Coalitions among different classes had flourished only for a short time after 1968. Social and economic interests were articulated directly to the state but in disparate channels. Meanwhile, voters still functioned within the context of loyalties and participation patterns controlled by the political parties. Any modern, reformist political movement had to contend with the proliferation of new interest groups, multiple lines of communication, and the inertia of customary alliances.

The fragmentation of political power and fluidity of social relations were unstable conditions, although the power of the state became evident as it acquired greater resources and assumed more economic and social roles. Regardless, the old system of caudillo politics by itself was unable to reestablish stability; personalistic rule and discipline had been undermined. These traits were crucial to the political parties, and as they were eroded, both the structure of the parties and the mode of governing were weakened. A political vacuum was formed between the faltering grasp on power by old elites and the untested political viability of urban middle-class and popular-sector groups. The dispersal of power among declining political institutions, emergent sociopolitical groups, and the potential military governors made the Honduran political system vulnerable to domestic unrest and external influences.

The vacuum of political power was gradually filled by the armed forces of Honduras. Though barely three decades old, the modern military has become the repository of political power. Its political role was initially that of arbitrator during the confused years of the early post-Carías era. At that juncture, the function of the armed forces was perceived mainly in terms of guaranteeing public order. During the early 1960s, the military's role was focused more on counterinsurgency and it came to view itself as the promoter of national security. Civic-action programs, for example, involved the army in activities nominally under control of civilian agencies. Eventually, the interests of the military institution were to become intertwined among the vicissitudes of civilian politics. A core of mutual background and interests created a political alliance between the military and the National party. This collaboration allowed the traditional elites (Nationalists) to stave off political demands of the progressive economic sectors and popular movements.

In many respects the evolution of the armed institution paralleled the rise of Oswaldo López Arellano to the head of the armed forces. The general and president of the republic had, in a sense, become another national caudillo—this time dressed in a military uniform. López Arellano and the armed forces adapted to the outline of caudillo politics, which enhanced the hold of the military on state and nation. Control over the state machinery brought numerous opportunities for personal gain and enrichment. In the style of caudillo politics, military factionalism, encouraged by dissident civilian groups that sought access to and favors from the state, reflected the desire of junior officers to share in the spoils of power. Under military rule, authority had once again been imposed upon the polity, but the roots of political instability were still nurtured by the transitional dynamics of state and society.

The 1969 war with El Salvador and the dismal failure of the National Unity government in 1972 were events that led the military from its role of political arbiter toward the assumption of direct rule. The alliance between military officers and National party stalwarts was shaken as the new sociopolitical sectors finally gained access to, and the support of, higher-ranking military leaders. Importantly, General López Arellano by then had perceived the evolving realignment of social and political forces. The inclusion of new political participants was necessary to preserve national stability and, at the same time, the military's newly established political power. Liberal and National party dissidents, relieved, joined the second government of López Arellano in support of national development policies. The momentum for reform lasted less than three years before the pattern of wider participation and popular access was reversed.

From 1972 to 1982, the Honduran political system was ruled by military officers. At first, high-level access on the part of conservative elements was limited. As leadership shifted from the personalism of López Arellano toward the more collegial form of the Superior Council of the Armed Forces, the military governors became more receptive to traditional elites. Civil-military relations oriented around the National party and the conservative ranching interests regained some of their customary influence.

Military intervention into the Honduran political process and the assumption of a governing role was accomplished in collaboration with different civilian political factions. In each coup (1956, 1963, and 1972), the armed forces had been encouraged to intervene either by dissident factions of the National party, isolated Liberals, or—in 1972—the peasant and labor unions associated with the Confederation of Honduran Workers.

The shifting coalitions among civilian political groups and the military have demonstrated the permeability and flexibility of the Honduran armed forces. Policy shifts have occurred in response to political realignments and the constellation of rising and falling military factions. The Honduran military is not a monolithic institution nor is it isolated from domestic and political pressures. Indeed, the military, even as its institutional identity has increased, has remained amenable to the temptations of corruption, especially as it has served the interests of personal gain and functioned to maintain political dominance.

The military "political elites" utilized their control over the state apparatus in much the same way that Honduran political elites had during the 1900s, 1920s, and later. Industry, modernized commercial agriculture, and employment with the transnational corporations provided few options for the upwardly mobile middle-class and upper-class social strata. Young professionals, technocrats, and educated military officers viewed government with its expanding resource base as a fount of economic well-being and personal advancement. The forms of Honduran traditional politics were being accepted by new generations whose futures were not particularly linked with those of the traditional political parties and the former system of caudillo politics.

No consensus ever developed among military leaders as to whether or not to mobilize Hondurans in support of the military governments. General López Arellano, however, toyed with the idea of consolidating his position at the head of a "populist" regime. This plan, if ever seriously considered, engendered angry conservative resistance in addition to opposition within CONSUFFAA. During this period (the 1970s), the nascent collegial form of leadership worked against personal aggrandizement by individual military officers. Similarly, the dismissal of General Melgar Castro occurred as the chief of state sought to transform and parlay his personal ambition and popularity into a broad-based political movement. Conservative civilian opponents and ambitious colonels within CONSUFFAA blocked Melgar Castro's dream of being an elected president of the republic. Gen. Policarpo Paz García also became enamored with the presidency and the possibility of somehow maneuvering within the electoral process so that the military leader could be elected president.

THE CYCLE OF FRUSTRATION

Throughout the post-Carías era, the Honduran political system has had to contend with pressures for reform and participation. Without being overly prescriptive, if economic development and long-term political stability are considered national objectives, progress toward national political integration would appear to serve Hondurans well in reaching those goals. At issue is the eventual form and composition of national unity and the direction that the country's economic and social development might take.

Physical, historical, and socioeconomic barriers to Honduran integration have been partially overcome by measurable progress in national development. The extension of roads, more educational opportunities, steps taken to create industrial capacity, and the minimal but continuing spread of literacy have enhanced national communication among regions and differing social classes. Economic transformation has breached some of the divisions between traditional society and the enclave development along the North Coast. Nevertheless some form of institutionalized accommodation to persistent demands has yet to be fully achieved. The cycle of political openings followed by political demobilization has alternatively raised popular expectations and instilled cynicism among nontraditional sociopolitical forces, and in some instances, even within the ranks of the traditional political parties.

In recent times, the 1969 war with El Salvador incited national patriotic fervor in which all Hondurans could unabashedly participate. Whether the conflict was encouraged by anxious political elites in an effort to diffuse political tensions or not, the response of most Hondurans resulted in a rare sense of national pride and unity. Only six years later, the 1975 bribery case involving López Arellano and the United Brands company brought disparate political sectors together in response to the international scandal.

Another series of national experiences has been the periodic elections. Misconduct of many national and local elections has often perpetuated political divisions. Political violence, abuse of voters, and the maneuvers associated with the historical political parties have undermined the legitimacy of several Honduran governments. On the other hand, for most Hondurans, voting is the most concrete form of participation within the political system. The number and proportion of eligible citizens registered to vote has increased steadily since the 1920s. High turnouts characterized the 1980 and 1981 elections, and both were deemed "civic fiestas."

The perceptible beginnings of national integration are, however, far from reaching levels of sustained viability. Despite progress made in economic development, there remain serious deficiencies as demonstrated by the lack of adequate housing, malnutrition, and high infant mortality rates. Political differences are intense over issues of agrarian reform, the extent of social and economic reform, and the nature of civil-military relations.

In some respects, the so-called weaknesses of Honduras may be an advantage for the country's mid-term success in socioeconomic development. The Honduras of the early 1980s was a less polarized society than El Salvador or Guatemala. Despite more than a decade of military rule, the polity was not burdened by an isolated and concentrated power elite such as that illustrated by the Somoza dynasty in Nicaragua. Extensive poverty and maldistribution of income are overbearing problems. Antagonisms between rich and poor exist and will most likely worsen. Yet, the range of disparity among social strata in Honduras has been less than that of other Latin American countries. Sometimes this is called the "democracy of poverty." In a similar vein, the diluted sense of "aristocracy," while perhaps a historical disadvantage to national integration, represents another aspect of political flexibility. The absence of an isolated, retrograde oligarchy contributes to reduced levels of social polarization. At the same time, it contributes to facets of pluralistic development as elites tend to be more amenable to influence by multiple and diverse interests.

The lingering aspects of traditional social forms and relationships also help sustain the intimacy of Honduran society. Importantly, Hondurans retain the ability to talk with one another. Political opponents are able to function together, though imperfectly. However, signs of externally influenced terror and insurrection and excessive physical coercion by public authorities have appeared. These are phenomena that tend to subvert the familiarity of Honduran social relations by inducing mistrust and fear.

The irony of the Honduran political system is that the historical political parties may still represent one resource by which the country might resolve some of its basic political problems. Required, however, is the melding of an objective analysis of the Honduran social, economic, and political situation with the networks of personal ties and patron-client relations that are basic to Liberal and National party organizations. The objectives of national development and security might be enhanced if the more positive and functional aspects of caudillo politics were utilized to broaden the scope of citizen participation. Such an inclusionary course of action would require extensive revision of attitudes and perspectives on the part of the traditional ruling groups, party activists, and military leaders.

The cycle of political frustration stems from unresolved social and economic issues, intractable problems of development, and periodic exclusionary politics. These factors help to exacerbate contemporary political differences; and fragmentation of the polity in turn hinders efforts to transform traditional economic and social structures and to promote institutional development that would then facilitate national integration. Resistance by traditional elites has inhibited political change and the development of widely accepted ways to resolve conflict, but the military rulers share the responsibility for these shortcomings along with the leadership of the Liberal and National political parties. Disruption of the cycle eventually depends upon long-term social and economic development. Socioeconomic progress and political stability could help moderate anxieties of the military governors while strengthening civilian political institutions. Successful and effective performance of the government would also mitigate doubts about civilian intentions and governing capacities.

Since 1950, the false starts of political openings and expanded social participation have jolted Hondurans as progressive regimes lost the ability or the nerve to sustain reformist policies. When popular demands were strongly articulated, some access to power was gained, but governmental responses have fallen woefully short time and time again. The effectiveness of any national development program will be tied to the resolution of the country's crucial political issues. Until the circle of socioeconomic fragmentation, political frustration, and lack of national integration is broken, the vulnerability of the Honduran polity to domestic unrest and outside intervention will be paramount. Barriers to integration can be eliminated to the extent possible by reducing physical, social, and economic divisions. Levels of public frustration can be lowered by opening the political process and improving governmental responses to the most critical issues of national development. Vulnerability of the regime could also be mitigated by promoting fairer election practices, working toward less corrupt officialdom, and retreating from the beginnings of official violence.

It is unrealistic to expect Honduras to evolve toward a democratic system based upon classical principles of individualism. The country's cultural heritage, hierarchial social structure, and centralized patterns of authority would suggest more collective forms of social and political interaction. For example, the proliferation of organized interest groups and the appearance of new political movements have left organic bases upon which public participation could be expanded. Honduran politics is a mixture of the old and new. The political style of caudillos supported by traditional cultural patterns persists alongside the search for stable and efficient patterns of government. A combination of new political vision and older institutions could encourage the promotion of younger, progressive leaders to positions of influence within the traditional political parties. It could also imply a broadened agenda of political debate that included new political movements and other forms of public participation. Such a course for Honduran political development is fraught with uncertainty and even dangers. But it is questionable whether the old-guard elites, even within the context of the Central American crisis, would willingly support serious structural change or permit new political leaders to acquire power without a struggle. Absent some type of accommodation to social and economic change, new political leadership will emerge but in unexpected or more radical ways. The crisis in Central America has drastically narrowed the time frame for Hondurans to devise solutions to both their old and future political problems.

Notes

CHAPTER 1

1. See Edgardo Quiñónez and Mario Argueta, *História de Honduras* (Tegucigalpa, D.C.: Escuela Superior del Profesorado "Francisco Morazán," 1978), pp. 58 ff. Cf. Franklin D. Parker, *The Central American Republics* (New York: Oxford University Press, 1964), pp. 75–89.

2. See Gene Alan Muller, "The Church in Poverty: Bishops, Bourbons, and Tithes in Spanish Honduras, 1700–1821" (Ph.D dissertation, University of Kansas, 1981).

3. Guillermo Molina Chocano, *Estado Liberal y desarrollo capitalista en Honduras* (Tegucigalpa, D.C.: Banco Central de Honduras, 1976); Ciro F. S. Cardoso and Héctor Pérez Brignoli, *Centro América y la economía occidental (1520–1930)* (San José: Editorial de la Universidad de Costa Rica, 1977), pp. 295 ff.; and José Reina Valenzuela and Mario Argueta, *Marco Aurelio Soto: Reforma Liberal de 1876* (Tegucigalpa, D.C.: Banco Central de Honduras, 1978).

4. Guillermo Molina Chocano, "La formación del estado y el origen minero-mercantil de la burguesia hondureña," *Estudios sociales centroamericanos* 9, no. 25 (January–April 1980), p. 67. Cf. the detailed works by Kenneth V. Finney, "Rosario and the Election of 1887: The Political Economy of Mining in Honduras," *Hispanic American Historical Review* 59, no. 1 (February 1979), pp. 81–107, and "Precious Metal Mining and the Modernization of Honduras: In Quest of El Dorado (1880–1900)" (Ph.D dissertation, Tulane University, 1973).

In 1887–1888, more than half of Honduran exports were minerals. Of this, Rosario's share was near 90 percent. See Víctor Meza and Héctor López, "Las inversiones extranjeras en Honduras antes del Mercado Común Centroamericano," *Economía política*, no. 6 (1973).

5. A multitude of articles, books, monographs, and other essays provide an ample but often biased picture of the origins, impact, and consequences of the banana industry in Central America and Honduras. See Charles David Kepner, Jr., and Jay Henry Soothill, *The Banana Empire: A Case Study of Economic Imperialism* (New York: Russell and Russell, 1967); also see Charles David Kepner, Jr., *Social Aspects of the Banana Industry* (New York: AMS Press, 1967). Others are Frederick Upham Adams, *Conquest of the Tropics: The Story of Creative*

Enterprise Conducted by the United Fruit Company (New York: Arno Press, 1976); Thomas L. Karnes, *The Tropical Enterprise: The Standard Fruit and Steamship Company in Latin America* (Baton Rouge: Louisiana State University Press, 1978); Stacy May and Galo Plaza, *The United Fruit Company in Latin America* (Washington, D.C.: National Planning Association, 1958); and Charles Morrow Wilson, *Empire in Green and Gold: The Story of the American Banana Trade* (New York: Henry Holt and Company, 1947).

Honduran scholars have analyzed the epoch more critically. See especially Vilma Lainez and Víctor Meza, "El enclave bananero en la história de Honduras," *Estudios sociales centroamericanos* 2, no. 5 (May–August 1973), pp. 115–156; Antonio Murga Frassinetti, *Enclave y sociedad en Honduras* (Tegucigalpa, D.C.: Universidad Nacional Autonoma de Honduras, 1978); and Mario Posas A. and Rafael del Cid, *La construcción del sector público y del estado nacional de Honduras, 1876–1979* (San José: EDUCA, 1981).

For accounts after the 1975 "bananagate" affair, see Enrique Flores Valeriano, *La explotación bananera en Honduras* (Tegucigalpa, D.C.: Editorial Universitaria, 1979); Edmundo Valades, *Los contratos del diablo* (México: Editores Asociados, 1975); and Thomas P. McCann, *An American Company: The Tragedy of United Fruit* (New York: Crown Publishers, 1976).

A richly detailed study of the relationship between Honduran political leaders and the United Fruit Company is contained in Edward Boatman-Guillán, "The Political Role of the United Fruit Company in Honduras, 1890–1950" (draft of Ph.D dissertation, Johns Hopkins University, 1982). Also see the novels by Ramón A. Amador, *Prisión verde* (Tegucigalpa, D.C.: Editorial "Ramón Amaya-Amador," 1974), and O. Henry, *Cabbages and Kings* (Garden City, N.Y.: Doubleday, Page and Co., 1919).

6. See Jorge Morales, "El ferrocarril nacional de Honduras: su historia e incidencia sobre el desarrollo económico," *Estudios sociales centroamericanos* 1, no. 2 (May–August 1972), pp. 7–20.

7. See Mario Posas A., *Las sociedades artesanales y los orígenes del movimiento obrero hondureño* (San José: ESP Editorial, 1977).

8. See Julio Cotler, "State and Regime: Comparative Notes on the Southern Cone and the 'Enclave' Societies," in *The New Authoritarianism in Latin America,* edited by David Collier (Princeton: Princeton University Press, 1979), pp. 255–284; and Murga, op. cit.

9. Boatman-Guillán, op. cit., chap. 6.

10. For details about this period, see Robert Anthony White, "Structural Factors in Rural Development: The Church and Peasant in Honduras" (Ph.D dissertation, Cornell University, 1977), chap. 2; James A. Morris, "Interest-Groups and Politics in Honduras" (Ph.D dissertation, University of New Mexico, 1974); and Posas and del Cid, op. cit., chap. 2.

11. Guillermo Molina Chocano, "Población, estructura productiva, y migraciones internas en Honduras (1950–1960)," *Estudios sociales centroamericanos* 4, no. 12 (September–December 1975), p. 14.

12. As quoted in Stefan Baciu, *Ramón Villeda Morales: Ciudadano de América* (San José: Imprenta Antonio Lehmann, 1970), p. 28.

CHAPTER 2

1. *Desarrollo y aprovechamiento de los recursos humanos* (Tegucigalpa, D.C.: Consejo Superior de Planificación Económico [CONSUPLANE], June 1980), p. 9.

2. *Central American Report* (Guatemala) 8, nos. 6 and 27 (7 February and 11 July 1981).

3. Robert W. Fox and Jerrold W. Huguet, *Population and Urban Trends in Central America and Panama* (Washington, D.C.: Inter-American Development Bank, 1977), pp. 136, 149.

4. *Desarrollo y aprovechamiento de los recursos humanos*, op. cit., pp. 33–35.

5. *Diagnóstico de los recursos humanos, 1961–1974* (Tegucigalpa, D.C.: CONSUPLANE, July 1976), p. 68. This standard was defined as "those who live on the edge of malnutrition, those for whom relatively minor changes in income, food prices, health status, family size, or environment conditions create significant hardship." See U.S. Agency for International Development (USAID), *Honduras: Country Development Strategy, FY 82* (Washington, D.C.: Government Printing Office, January 1980), pp. 2–3.

A survey in 1967-1968 found that 80 percent of the population received only 32 percent of the nation's income. Average annual income levels were on the order of fifty-four dollars per person. See Dirección General de Estadística y Censos (DGEC), *Encuesta de ingresos y gastos familiares, 1967/1968* (Tegucigalpa, D.C.: Ministerio de Economia, 1970); and James F. Torres, "Income Levels, Income Distribution, and Levels of Living in Rural Honduras: A Summary and Evaluation of Quantitative and Qualitative Data" (prepared for U.S. Department of Agriculture, Office of International Cooperation, River Falls, Wis., May 1979).

6. See Howard I. Blutstein et al., *Area Handbook for Honduras* (Washington, D.C.: American University, 1971), pp. 58 ff.; and Richard N. Adams, *Cultural Surveys of Panama–Nicaragua–Guatemala–El Salvador–Honduras* (Washington, D.C.: Pan American Sanitary Bureau, 1957), pp. 607 ff.

7. Nancie L. González-Solien, *Black Carib Household Structure: A Study of Migration and Modernization* (Seattle: University of Washington Press, 1969), chaps. 2 and 3.

8. See Gene Alan Muller, "The Church in Poverty: Bishops, Bourbons, and Tithes in Spanish Honduras, 1700–1821" (Ph.D. dissertation, University of Kansas, 1981).

9. See Kenneth G. Grub, *Religion in Central America* (New York: World Dominion Press, 1937), chap. 6; and Robert Anthony White, "Structural Factors in Rural Development: The Church and Peasant in Honduras" (Ph.D. dissertation, Cornell University, 1977), pp. 105–106.

10. Robert A. White, *Mass Communications and the Popular Promotion Strategy of Rural Development in Honduras* (Stanford: Institute for Communication Research, 1976), pp. 17 ff.

11. The number of students in higher education increased more than tenfold in fifteen years—from twenty-six hundred university students in 1965 to nearly twenty-four thousand in 1980.

12. Adams, op. cit., pp. 572 ff.

13. See Guillermo Molina Chocano, "Población, estructura productiva, y migraciones internas en Honduras (1950–1960)," *Estudios sociales centroamericanos* 4, no. 12 (September–December 1975), pp. 9–39. Also, Confederación Universitaria Centroamericana (CSUCA)/Programa Centroamericano de Ciencias Sociales, *Estructura demográfica y migraciones internas en Centroamerica* (San José:

EDUCA, 1978), chap. 4; and Jorge Arévalo, *Migraciones: Encuesta demográfica nacional de Honduras, Fascile V* (Santiago: Centro Latinoamericano de Demografía, October 1975).

14. Fox and Huguet, op. cit., pp. 22–33.

CHAPTER 3

1. Lucas Paredes, *Los culpables (ensayo biográfico)* (Tegucigalpa, D.C.: Imprenta Honduras, 1970), pp. 230 ff.

2. Velásquez Cerrato, though frustrated, remained politically active. In 1981 he campaigned for office under the National party's banner, and in 1983 President Suazo Córdova appointed him ambassador to Spain.

3. Republic of Honduras, *Constitution of 1957*, Article 319.

4. Lucas Paredes, *Liberalismo y nacionalismo (Transfugísmo político)* (Tegucigalpa, D.C.: Imprenta Honduras, 1963), p. 383.

5. Documents of the Confederation of Honduran Workers (CTH), "SITRATERCO Strike Declaration" (18 September 1968).

6. Confederación de Trabajadores de Honduras, "Llamamiento del sindicalismo hondureño a la conciencia nacional" (II Asamblea Nacional Ordinaria, Ponencia no. 9, 22 March 1969). Cf. Secretario Ejecutivo del Consejo Superior de Planificación Económico (CONSUPLANE), "Memorandum sobre obstáculos al desarrollo" (Tegucigalpa, D.C., 15 June 1967).

7. "Necesidad de análizar los problemas nacionales y obligación de buscarles soluciones," speech given by Oscar Gale Varela before the III Reunión de la Fuerzas Vivas de Honduras (21 November 1969).

8. Article 4 of the 1965 constitution states in part that "Integration implies participation by all social, economic, and political sectors in public administration, a principle that authorities must respect in order to insure and strengthen Honduran nationality, and to make viable the progress of Honduras based upon political stability and national conciliation." República de Honduras, *Constitución de la República* (Decreto No. 20 de la Asamblea Nacional Constituyente, 1965).

9. See James A. Morris, *The Honduran Plan Político de Unidad Nacional, 1971–1972: Its Origins and Demise,* occasional paper (El Paso: Center for Inter-American Studies, University of Texas at El Paso, 1975).

10. *El Tiempo* (2 May 1972).

CHAPTER 4

1. Diogenes Lempira, "Las nuevas fuerzas polítcas," *El Tiempo* (7 February 1973). Cf. Rafael Leiva Vivas, *Vacio político, crisis general, y alternativas al desarrollo* (n. p., 1975).

2. *La Prensa* (30 March 1973).

3. See *Wall Street Journal* (9, 11, and 14 April 1975).

4. *New York Times* (25 April 1975).

5. ANACH, UNC, and the Federation of Agrarian Reform Cooperatives of Honduras (FECORAH) formed the Frente de Unidad Campesina in order to collectively pressure the government on matters of agrarian reform. See *El Tiempo* (11 October 1975).

6. Benjamín Santos M., *Díez años de lucha: Partido Demócrata Cristiano de Honduras* (Guatemala: Editorial INCEP, 1980), p. 279.

7. The Liberals won thirty-five seats to the National party's thirty-three.

8. See James A. Morris, "Honduras: How Long an Oasis of Peace?" *Caribbean Review* 8, no. 1 (Winter 1981), pp. 38–41.

9. *Latin American Regional Report: Mexico and Central America* (5 June 1981).

10. Víctor Meza, "El Frente Patriotico Hondureño y las elecciones," *El Tiempo* (11 July 1981).

11. The eighty-two seats of the National Congress were distributed among the PLH (forty-four), the PNH (thirty-four), PINU (three), and the PDCH (one).

12. *La Tribuna* (28 January 1982).

CHAPTER 5

1. In 1983, cabinet-level agencies included Government and Justice; Foreign Relations; Defense and Public Security; Economy and Commerce; Finance and Public Credit; Public Education; Public Health and Social Welfare; Labor and Social Provision; Communications, Public Works, and Transportation; Natural Resources; Culture and Tourism; and the Superior Council of Economic Planning. See Figure 5.1.

2. See *Manual de organizaciones y funciones de los organismos decentralizados* (Tegucigalpa, D.C.: Consejo Superior de Planificación Económico [CONSUPLANE], 1977).

3. Steve C. Ropp, "Transformation of the Honduran State: 1925–1976" (Central American Working Group paper, New Mexico State University, 1978). Also see Joseph R. Thompson, "An Economic Analysis of the Public Expenditure in Honduras, 1925–1963" (Ph.D. dissertation, University of Florida, 1968).

4. República de Honduras, *Presupuesto general de ingresos y egresos de la República: Integrada por programas*, Gobierno Central, ejercicio fiscal de 1979 (Tegucigalpa, D.C.: Ministerio de Hacienda y Credito Público, 1979). Budgets during the early 1980s reflected similar distribution of resources. One significant departure was the maintenance of the defense budget at the same level for three years. This occurred, however, during a period when U.S. military aid and credits were being extended by the United States at increasing rates.

5. During the first year of the Suazo government (1982), several thousand public employees were laid off or dismissed. In part this reflected attempts to reduce the expenditures of the central government and lower the budgetary deficits. However, it appeared that most of the former civil servants were National party followers, and in many cases, they were replaced by Liberal party supporters.

6. Ubodoro Arriaga, "El poder de la asamblea nacional constituyente," *Relieve* (December 1979), p. 6.

7. See República de Honduras, *Ley de Municipalidades y del Regimen Político* (9 April 1927), and subsequent amendments and revisions.

8. CONSUPLANE, "Estructura actual del sístema de planificación y coordinación regional y local de la Secretaría Tecnica del Consejo Superior de Planificación Económica" (Tegucigalpa, D.C., December 1979), p. 15.

9. See Asamblea Nacional Constituyente, *Ley electoral y de las organizaciones políticas*, Decreto No. 53 (Tegucigalpa, D.C.: República de Honduras, 20 April 1981).

10. James A. Morris, "Honduran Elections and Patterns of Party Support" (Central American Working Group paper, New Mexico State University, June 1982).

CHAPTER 6

1. George Philip, "The Military Institution Revisited: Some Notes on Corporatism and Military Rule in Latin America," *Journal of Latin American Studies* 12, no. 2 (November 1980), p. 422.

2. See Benjamín Santos M., *Díez años de lucha: Partido Demócrata Cristiano de Honduras* (Guatemala: Editorial INCEP, 1980).

3. Partido Revolucionario de Honduras, "Declaración de principios del PRH," *Nueva sociedad*, no. 33 (November–December 1977), pp. 182–190.

4. The FPH was organized in 1979, grouping together the Honduran Marxist left and other popular-sector organizations such as student groups, teacher associations, and recently formed peasant and labor associations. After the 1980 elections, the Marxist-oriented groups, including the Communist party (PCH), contested the front's leadership by the Christian Democrats. But in 1981, once the PDCH acquired its legal status, the Christian Democrats withdrew from the FPH.

5. See Steve C. Ropp, "Honduras," in *Yearbook on International Communist Affairs, 1983*, edited by Richard F. Staar (Stanford: Hoover Institution Press, 1983). For more background, see the essays by Neale J. Pearson in the 1981 and 1982 yearbooks.

6. Cf. James A. Morris and Steve C. Ropp, "Corporatism and Dependent Development: A Honduran Case Study," *Latin American Research Review* 12, no. 2 (Summer 1977), pp. 27–68; and Robert Anthony White, "Structural Factors in Rural Development: The Church and Peasant in Honduras" (Ph.D. dissertation, Cornell University, 1977), Appendix.

7. See Vinicio González, "La insurrección salvadoreña de 1932 y la gran huelga hondureña de 1954," *Revista méxicana de sociologia* 40, no. 2 (April–June 1978), pp. 563–606; Víctor Meza, *Historia del movimiento obrero hondureño* (Tegucigalpa, D.C.: Editorial Guaymuras, 1980); and Mario Posas A., *Lucha ideologica y organización sindical en Honduras (1954–65)* (Tegucigalpa, D.C.: Editorial Guaymuras, 1980). Also see Robert Lee MacCameron, *Bananas, Labor, and Politics in Honduras: 1954–1963*, Foreign and Comparative Studies/Latin American Series, no. 5 (Syracuse, N.Y.: Maxwell School of Citizenship and Public Affairs, Syracuse University, 1983).

8. See James A. Morris and Marta Sánchez, "Factores de poder en la evolución política del campesinado hondureño," *Estudios sociales centroamericanos* 6, no. 16 (January–April 1977), pp. 85–106.

9. The most important teacher associations are the Honduran Teachers for Professional Improvement (COLPROSUMAH), First Honduran Professional Association of Teachers (PRICHMA), the Honduran Association of Secondary Teachers (COPEMH), and the Colegio Union Magisterial (CUM). In 1980, the several groups formed the Teacher's Unity Front (FUM).

10. Much of the information and some analysis is taken from the extensive work of Robert Anthony White, op. cit., pp. 190–325.

11. See *Reflexión sobre la formación de la conciencia política* (Santa Rosa de Copán: Diócesis de Santa Rosa de Copán, January 1979). Also see the various pastoral letters issued by the Honduran bishops; e.g., see *La Tribuna* (28 October 1982).

12. Treaties and documents still in force were signed in 1950, 1952, 1954, 1956, 1962, 1972 and 1975. See U.S. Department of State, *Treaties in Force*

(Washington, D.C.: Government Printing Office, 1979), pp. 84–85. Another agreement was signed in 1982 formalizing U.S. military-aid programs.

13. Steve C. Ropp, "The Honduran Army in the Sociopolitical Evolution of the Honduran State," *The Americas* 30, no. 4 (April 1974), pp. 504–528.

14. *Ley Constitutiva de las Fuerzas Armadas de Honduras,* Decreto No. 180, 30 January 1975 (Tegucigalpa, D.C.: Departamento de Relaciones Públicas, 1975). Also see the appropriate articles in the constitutions of 1957, 1965, and 1982.

CHAPTER 7

1. See Elizabeth E. Eldridge and Denis R. Rydjeski, "Algunos aspectos de las inversiones estadounidenses en Honduras," *Economía política,* no. 2 (July–September 1972), pp. 66–79.

2. For a cogent analysis of the dual economic structure and its relationship to foreign investment, see Guillermo Molina Chocano, "Dependencia y cambio social en la sociedad hondureña," *Estudios sociales centroamericanos* 1, no. 1 (January–April 1972), pp. 11–26.

3. *Yearbook of International Trade Statistics,* vol. 1, *Trade by Country* (New York: United Nations, 1979), p. 448. For 1980, Honduran imports (by value) were machinery and transport (29.2 percent), diverse manufactured articles (27.3 percent), chemicals (15.2 percent), and combustibles (16.8 percent). The remainder was mostly food imports (9.9 percent).

4. See Marta Reina de Argueta, "Reseña histórica del Sistema Bancario de Honduras, 1868–1950," *Mundo BANTRAL,* ed. extraordinaria (Tegucigalpa, D.C., July 1976). "In effect, before this date [1949], North American money circulated due to the growing demands for currency which made it necessary to import it, despite the fact that the lempira had been authorized to circulate in April 1926. With the establishment of the Central Bank in 1950, the rising demand was eventually met . . . , the use of national currency was promoted, and the lempira was rescued from being overwhelmed by the dollar."

5. *Imagen de la estructura económica-social y explotación de los recursos naturales* (Tegucigalpa, D.C.: Consejo Superior de Planificación Económico [CON-SUPLANE], 1973), pp. 66 ff. Also see *Boletín del IIES,* no. 81 (Tegucigalpa, D.C.: UNAH, March 1979).

6. See *Incentivos fiscales al desarrollo industrial: evaluación de su aplicación en Honduras, 1958–1971* (Tegucigalpa, D.C.: Banco Central de Honduras [BAN-TRAL], July 1972).

7. See *Central American Report* 9, no. 37 (24 September 1982); and *La Nación Internacional* (San José) (16–22 December 1982).

8. See *Latin American Weekly Report* (London) (8 October 1982); and *La Nación Internacional* (27 January–2 February 1983).

9. See "Central American Energy," *South, The Third World Magazine* (June 1981), pp. 69–71.

10. José Miguel Velloso, "Who Cares for the Forest?" *Ceres* 14, no. 14 (July–August 1981), pp. 40–43.

11. The 1974 survey was conducted scarcely a year after Decree Law No. 8 had been issued and before the 1975 Agrarian Reform Law had been decreed. According to INA figures, only 36,000 hectares had been distributed since 1962, and fewer than 33,000 hectares were adjudicated during all of 1974. Therefore, the impact of the "reformed sector" on land-tenure patterns was minimal at

best. See Instituto Nacional Agrario, *Resumen de datos generales del sector reformado* (Tegucigalpa, D.C.: Departamento de Planificación, December 1978), p. 27.

12. Decree Law No. 2 (26 September 1962). See "Agrarian Reform Law in Honduras," *International Labour Review* 87, no. 6 (June 1963), pp. 573–580.

13. The peasant associations speak of recuperation or occupation, whereas the press, the large landowners, and the urban public refer to "invasions." Other than the political overtones attached to the terms, there is some distinction to be made between them. Land occupation is viewed by the peasant movement as a tactic applied to national or *ejidal* (communal) lands, whereas land invasions are directed at known private lands to produce a crisis situation. Of course the landowners perceive any such actions as invasions even if the land occupied is national and has been illegally appropriated by an individual. Undoubtedly, this distinction leads to innumerable disputes as a result of unclear title histories and conflicting interpretations.

14. See James A. Morris, *The Honduran Plan Político de Unidad Nacional, 1971–1972: Its Origins and Demise*, occasional paper (El Paso: Center for Inter-American Studies, University of Texas at El Paso, February 1975); and Mario Posas A., "Política estatal y estructura agraria en Honduras (1950–1978)," *Estudios sociales centroamericanos* 8, no. 24 (September–December 1979), pp. 75–76.

15. Figures from INA as published in *El Tiempo* (17 February 1975), and from Gustavo Adolfo Hernández, *Problematica de las cooperativas en los programas de la reforma agraria en Centro América*, no. 24 (Tegucigalpa, D.C.: PROCCARA-INA, 1978). One *manzana* is equal to 0.69 hectare or 1.72 acres.

16. The Union of Banana Exporting Countries (UPEB) includes Honduras, Panama, Costa Rica, Guatemala, Nicaragua, Colombia, the Dominican Republic, and Venezuela. Honduras ratified the agreement in September 1975.

17. See *Wall Street Journal* (9, 11, and 14 April 1975); and *New York Times* (13 and 24 April 1975).

18. Consejo Asesor del Jefe del Estado sobre la Política Bananera Nacional, "Informe final," (July 1975) as published in Enrique Flores Valeriano, *La explotación bananera en Honduras* (Tegucigalpa, D.C.: Editorial Universitaria, 1979), pp. 47–73.

19. See Daniel Slutzky and Esther Alonso, *Empresas transnacionales y agricultura: El caso del enclave bananero en Honduras* (Tegucigalpa, D.C.: Editorial Universitaria, 1980), annexes.

20. *World Bank Annual Report, 1981*, p. 138. The figure for Honduras is not overly excessive but does indicate a disturbing trend, especially in the context of an economic downturn. It does, however, compare favorably with that of Costa Rica (23.1 percent), Brazil (34.6 percent), and Mexico (64.1 percent), although the diverse economic structures must be considered. On the other hand, Guatemala (2.2 percent) and El Salvador (3.2 percent) have maintained a steadier debt-service ratio.

21. Figures for this discussion of Honduran trade derived from data contained in Dirección General de Estadística y Censos (DGEC), *Compendio estadístico, 1966/1967* and *Compendio estadístico, 1977*, and BANTRAL, *Honduras en cifras, 1978–1980* (Tegucigalpa, D.C.: Departamento de Estudios Económicos, 1981).

CHAPTER 8

1. Among the numerous works on the Central American Common Market and the process of economic integration, see Isaac Cohen Orantes, *Regional Integration in Central America* (Lexington, Mass.: D. C. Heath, 1972); Mitchell Seligson, "Transactions and Community Formation: Fifteen Years of Growth and Stagnation in the CACM," *Journal of Common Market Studies* 5, no. 3 (March 1967); and Royce Q. Shaw, *Central America: Regional Integration and National Political Development* (Boulder, Colo.: Westview Press, 1978).

2. *Comercio exterior* (México) 29, no. 6 (June 1976).

3. See John Saxe-Fernández, "El Consejo de Defensa Centroamericano y la Pax Americana," *Cuadernos americanos* 152, no. 3 (May–June 1967), pp. 39–57; and Laun C. Smith Jr., "Central American Defense Council: Some Problems and Achievements," *Air University Review* (March–April 1969), pp. 67–75.

4. For only a few studies about the conflict, see Vincent Cable, "The Football War and the Central American Common Market," *International Affairs* 45, no. 4 (October 1969), pp. 658–671; Marco Virgilio Carías and Daniel Slutzky, *La guerra inútil: análisis socioeconómico del conflicto entre Honduras y El Salvador* (San José: Editorial Universitaria Centroamericana [EDUCA], 1971); Caleb Clark and Steve C. Ropp, *Disintegrative Tendencies in the Central American Common Market*, occasional papers (Tucson: Institute of Government Research, University of Arizona, 1974); and William H. Durham, *Scarcity and Survival in Central America: Ecological Origins of the Soccer War* (Stanford: Stanford University Press, 1979).

5. See, for example, Steve C. Ropp, "Cuba and Panama: Signaling Left and Going Right," *Caribbean Review* 9, no. 1 (Winter 1980); and Mitchell Seligson and William Carroll III, "The Costa Rican Role in the Sandinista Victory," in *Nicaragua in Revolution*, edited by Thomas W. Walker (New York: Praeger, 1982).

6. Estimates by Honduran officials in mid-1981 indicated twenty-five thousand refugees from El Salvador. United Nations estimates were higher (thirty thousand); other figures ranged as high as fifty thousand. Honduran data also included ten thousand people from Nicaragua plus three thousand Miskito Indians from the northeastern part of Nicaragua.

7. See *Washington Post* (16 March 1982); *New York Times* (20 April 1982); *Latin American Regional Report; Mexico and Central America* (13 August 1982); *Central American Report* 9, no. 33 (27 August 1982); *Newsweek Magazine* (8 November 1982); and Alan Riding, "The Central American Quagmire," *Foreign Affairs* 61, no. 3 (1983), pp. 648–649. Also see chapters by Jan Knippers Black and Jack C. Child in *Nicaragua, A Country Study*, edited by James D. Rudolph (Washington, D.C.: American University), pp. 181–182, 218–221.

8. See the testimony by Lt. Col. John H. Buchanan, U.S. Marine Corps (Retired), in U.S. Congress, House, Committee on Foreign Affairs, "Honduras and U.S. Policy: An Emerging Dilemma," *Hearing*, 97th Congress, 2d session (21 September 1982).

9. *Central American Report* 9, no. 46 (26 November 1982).

10. See *Central American Report* 9, no. 41 (22 October 1982).

11. See U.S. Department of State, *Department of State Bulletin* (December 1982).

12. "Agreement on Energy Cooperation Program for the Countries of Central America and the Caribbean" (San José, Costa Rica, 3 August 1980).

13. The Dominican Republic in 1965 might be raised as a successful example of such a situation of massive military intervention to control the immediate situation, followed by copious amounts of bilateral aid and investment. Since then, however, the position of the United States in global politics has been altered. Nor is Honduras geographically as ideal as was the island of Hispaniola. Another factor is the political consequences within the United States that such action might entail.

Conversion Chart For Measurements

To convert:	To:	Multiply by:
Manzanas	Acres	1.72
Manzanas	Hectares	0.70
Hectares	Acres	2.47
Hectares	Manzanas	1.43
Acres	Hectares	0.40
Acres	Manzanas	0.58
Kilometers	Miles	0.62
Miles	Kilometers	1.69
Sq. Kilometers	Sq. Miles	0.40
Sq. Miles	Sq. Kilometers	2.59
Millimeters	Inches	0.04
Inches	Millimeters	25.00

Abbreviations

ACPHO	Honduran Popular Cultural Action Agency
AHIBA	Honduran Association of Banking and Insurance Institutions
ALIPO	Popular Liberal Alliance
ANACH	National Association of Honduran Peasants
ANC	National Constituent Assembly
ANDI	National Association of Industries
BANADESA	National Development Bank
BANTRAL	Central Bank of Honduras
	Banco Central de Honduras
CACM	Central American Common Market
CCIA	Atlántida Chamber of Commerce
CCIC	Cortés Chamber of Commerce
CDC	Central American Democratic Community
CELADE	Latin American Demographic Center
CES	Special Security Forces
CETTNA	Centro Tecnico Tipo-Litográfico Nacional
CGT	General Central of Workers
CLAT	Latin American Central of Workers
COHBANA	Honduran Banana Corporation
COHDEFOR	Honduran Forestry Development Corporation
COHEP	Honduran Council of Private Enterprise
COLPROSUMAH	Honduran Teachers for Professional Improvement
CONADI	National Investment Corporation
CONASE	Presidential Advisory Council
CONCORDE	Coordinating Council for Development
CONDECA	Central American Defense Council
CONSUFFAA	Superior Council of the Armed Forces
CONSUPLANE	Superior Council of Economic Planning
	Consejo Superior de Planificación Económico
COPEMH	Honduran Association of Secondary Teachers

142

CORFINO	Forest Industry Corporation of Olancho
CSUCA	Confederación Universitaria Centroamericana
CTH	Confederation of Honduran Workers
CUM	Colegio Union Magisterial
DGEC	Dirección General de Estadística y Censos
EAP	economically active population
ECLA	Economic Commission for Latin America
EDUCA	Editorial Universitaria Centroamericana
ENEE	National Enterprise of Electrical Energy
ENP	National Port Enterprise
FECESITLIH	Central Federation of Free Worker Unions of Honduras
FECORAH	Federation of Agrarian Reform Cooperatives of Honduras
FENAGH	National Federation of Agriculturists and Stockraisers of Honduras
FESITRANH	Labor Federation of National Workers of Honduras
FMLH	Morazanist Front for the Liberation of Honduras
FNH	National Railroad of Honduras
FPH	Honduran Patriotic Front
FUL	Liberal Unity Front
FUM	Teacher's Unity Front
FUNACAMPH	National Unity Front of Honduran Peasants
GDP	gross domestic product
HONDUTEL	Honduran Telecommunications Enterprise
IDB	Inter-American Development Bank
IHAH	Honduran Institute of Anthropology and History
IHSS	Honduran Institute for Social Security
IMF	International Monetary Fund
INA	National Agrarian Institute
INFOP	Institute for Professional Development
INVA	Housing Institute
MNR	National Reformist Movement
MPL	Cinchonero Popular Liberation Movement
MUC	Movement of Unity and Change
NDP(s)	National Development Plan(s)
OAS	Organization of American States
ODECA	Organization of Central American States
OPEC	Organization of Petroleum Exporting Countries
ORIT	Inter-American Regional Organization of Workers
PASO	Socialist party
PCH	Communist Party of Honduras
PCH-ML	Communist Party of Honduras–Marxist-Leninist
PDCH	Christian Democratic party
PINU	Innovation and Unity party

PLH	Liberal Party of Honduras
PNH	National Party of Honduras
PRH	Honduran Revolutionary party
PRICHMA	First Honduran Professional Association of Teachers
PUN	National Unity party
SAHSA	Honduran Air Services
SITRATERCO	Union of the Tela Railroad Company Workers
SUTRASFCO	Unified Syndicate of Standard Fruit Company Workers
TNE	National Election Board
UN	United Nations
UNAH	Autonomous National University of Honduras
UNC	National Peasants Union
UPEB	Union of Banana Exporting Countries
URP	People's Revolutionary Union
USAID	U.S. Agency for International Development
USDA	U.S. Department of Agriculture

Selected Bibliography

BOOKS AND ARTICLES

Adams, Richard N. *Cultural Surveys of Panama–Nicaragua–Guatemala–El Salvador–Honduras.* Washington, D.C.: Pan American Sanitary Bureau, 1957.

"Agrarian Reform Law in Honduras." *International Labour Review* 87, no. 6 (June 1963), pp. 573–580.

Alvarez, A. "Evolución de la seguridad social en Honduras." *Estudios de la seguridad social* (Geneva) 5 (1973), pp. 20–30.

Alvarez, Diego, F. "Honduras: La reforma agraria del gobierno militar y las perspectivas en le gobierno constitucional." *Alcaraván*, no. 6 (January 1981), pp. 2–10.

Anderson, Charles W. "Honduras: Problems of an Apprentice Democracy." In *Political Systems of Latin America.* 2d ed., edited by Martin C. Needler. New York: Van Nostrand Reinhold Co., 1970, pp. 92–107.

Anderson, Thomas P. *Politics in Central America: Guatemala, El Salvador, Honduras, and Nicaragua.* Part 3. New York: Praeger, 1982.

Argueta, Mario. *Investigaciones y tendencias recientes de la historiografía hondureña: Un ensayo bibliográfico.* Colección Cuadernos Universitarios, no. 3. Tegucigalpa, D.C.: Editorial Universitaria, April 1981.

Argueta, Marta Reina de. "Reseña histórica del Sistema Bancario de Honduras," 1868–1950." *Mundo BANTRAL.* Ed. extraordinaria, July 1976.

Astorga Lira, Enrique. "Modelos marginales de reforma agraria en América Latina: El caso de Honduras." *Alcaraván*, no. 3 (April 1980), pp. 2–9.

Baciu, Stefan. *Ramón Villeda Morales: Ciudadano de América.* San José: Imprenta Antonio Lehmann, 1970.

Bardales, Rafael B. *Historia del Partido Nacional de Honduras.* Tegucigalpa, D.C.: Servicopiax Editores, 1980.

Barry, Tom; Beth Wood; and Deb Preusch. *Dollars and Dictators: A Guide to Central America.* Albuquerque: The Resource Center, 1982. Pp. 163–179.

Blutstein, Howard I., et al. *Area Handbook for Honduras.* Washington, D.C.: American University, 1971.

Boatman-Guillán, Edward. "The Political Role of the United Fruit Company in Honduras, 1890–1950." Draft, Ph.D. dissertation, Johns Hopkins University, 1982.

145

Cardoso, Ciro F. S., and Héctor Pérez Brignoli. *Centro América y la economía occidental (1520–1930)*. San José: Editorial de la Universidad de Costa Rica, 1977.

Carías, Marco Virgilio, and Daniel Slutzky. *La guerra inútil: Análisis socioeconómico del conflicto entre Honduras y El Salvador*. San José: Editorial Universitaria Centroamericana (EDUCA), 1971.

Chamberlain, Robert Stoner. *The Conquest and Colonization of Honduras, 1502–1550*. Washington, D.C.: Carnegie Institution of Washington, 1953.

Checchi, Vincent. *Honduras: A Problem in Economic Development*. New York: Twentieth Century Fund, 1959.

Cid, Rafael del. *Reforma agraria y capitalismo dependiente*. Tegucigalpa, D.C.: Editorial Universitaria, 1977.

Confederación Universitaria Centroamericana (CSUCA)/Programa Centroamericano de Ciencias Sociales. *Estructura demográfica y migraciones internas en Centroamerica*. San José: EDUCA, 1978.

"Constraints and Counterrevolution." *NACLA Report on the Americas* 16, no. 1 (January–February 1982), pp. 38–41.

Contreras, Carlos A. *Entre el marásmo: Análisis de la crisis del Partido Liberal de Honduras, 1933–1970*. Tegucigalpa, D.C.: HISA, 1970.

Díaz Zelaya, Rodolfo. *Algo más acerca de Honduras (Relaciones histórico, geográfico, turísticas)*. Tegucigalpa, D.C.: Centro Tecnico Tipo-Litográfico Nacional (CETTNA), 1978.

Domínguez, Raúl A., ed. *Ascenso al poder y descenso del General Oswaldo López Arellano*. Tegucigalpa, D.C.: Imprenta Calderón, 1975.

Durham, William H. *Scarcity and Survival in Central America: Ecological Origins of the Soccer War*. Stanford: Stanford University Press, 1979.

Durón, Rómulo E. *Bosquejo histórico de Honduras, 1502 a 1921*. San Pedro Sula: N. p., 1927.

Eldridge, Elizabeth E., and Denis R. Rydjeski. "Algunos aspectos de las inversiones estadounidenses en Honduras." *Economía política*, no. 2 (July–September 1972), pp. 66–79.

Ellis, Frank. "La valoración de exportaciones y las transferencias entre companias dedicadas a la industria de exportación en Centroamerica." *Estudios sociales centroamericanos* 8, no. 22 (January–April 1979), pp. 227–247.

Etchison, Don L. *The United States and Militarism in Central America*. New York: Praeger, 1975.

Fernández, Arturo. *Partidos políticos y elecciones en Honduras, 1980*. Tegucigalpa, D.C.: Editorial Guaymuras, 1981.

Finney, Kenneth V. "Rosario and the Election of 1887: The Political Economy of Mining in Honduras." *Hispanic American Historical Review* 59, no. 1 (February 1979), pp. 81–107.

Flores Valeriano, Enrique. *La explotación bananera en Honduras*. Tegucigalpa, D.C.: Editorial Universitaria, 1979.

Fox, Robert W., and Jerrold W. Huguet. *Population and Urban Trends in Central America and Panama*. Washington, D.C.: Inter-American Development Bank, 1977.

García, José Z. "Origins of Repressiveness or Moderation in the Militaries of El Salvador and Honduras." Paper presented at the Western Political Science Association meeting, San Diego, 25 March 1982.

González-Solien, Nancie L. *Black Carib Household Structure: A Study of Migration and Modernization*. Seattle: University of Washington Press, 1969.

Helms, Mary W. *Middle America: A Cultural History of Heartland and Frontiers.* Englewood Cliffs, N.J.: Prentice-Hall, 1975.

Karnes, Thomas L. *The Tropical Enterprise: The Standard Fruit and Steamship Company in Latin America.* Baton Rouge: Louisiana State University Press, 1978.

Kepner, Charles David, Jr., and Jay Henry Soothill. *The Banana Empire: A Case Study of Economic Imperialism.* New York: Russell and Russell, 1967.

Lainez, Vilma, and Víctor Meza. "El enclave bananero en la história de Honduras." *Estudios sociales centroamericanos* 2, no. 5 (May-August 1973), pp. 115–156.

Leiva Vivas, Rafael. *Un país en Honduras.* Tegucigalpa, D.C.: Imprenta Calderón, 1969.

––––––––. *Vacio político, crisis general, y alternativas al desarrollo.* N. p., 1975.

MacCameron, Robert Lee. *Bananas, Labor, and Politics in Honduras: 1954–1963.* Foreign and Comparative Studies/Latin American Series, no. 5. Syracuse, N.Y.: Maxwell School of Citizenship and Public Affairs, Syracuse University, 1983.

Mariñas Otero, Luis. *Honduras.* Madrid: Ediciones Cultura Hispánica, 1963.

Meyer, Harvey K. *Historical Dictionary of Honduras.* Latin American Historical Dictionaries, no. 13. Metuchen, N.J.: The Scarecrow Press, 1976.

Meza, Víctor. *Historia del movimiento obrero hondureño.* Tegucigalpa, D.C.: Editorial Guaymuras, 1980.

––––––––. "La trayectoria de la dependencia en Honduras." *El Tiempo Dominical* (3 February 1980).

––––––––. *Política y sociedad en Honduras.* Tegucigalpa, D.C.: Editorial Guaymuras, 1981.

––––––––. "Honduras en el marco de la estrategia económica de Washington." *Alcaraván,* no. 12 (April 1982), pp. 7–10.

Molina Chocano, Guillermo. "Dependencia y cambio social en la sociedad hondureña." *Estudios sociales centroamericanos* 1, no. 1 (January–April 1972), pp. 11–26.

––––––––. "La formación del estado y el origen minero-mercantil de la burguesia hondureña." *Estudios sociales centroamericanos* 9, no. 25 (January–April 1980), pp. 56–89.

––––––––. "Posibilidades y perspectivas del proceso de democratización en Honduras." *Nueva sociedad,* no. 48 (May–June 1980), pp. 79 ff.

Morris, James A. *The Honduran Plan Político de Unidad Nacional, 1971–1972: Its Origins and Demise.* Occasional Paper, Center for Inter-American Studies. El Paso: University of Texas at El Paso, February 1975.

––––––––. "Honduras: A Unique Case?" In *Latin American Politics and Development,* edited by Howard J. Wiarda and Harvey F. Kline. Boston: Houghton-Mifflin, 1979, pp. 346–357.

––––––––. "Honduras: How Long an Oasis of Peace?" *Caribbean Review* 8, no. 1 (Winter 1981), pp. 38–41.

––––––––. "Honduras." In *Political Parties of the Americas; Canada, Latin America, and the West Indies,* edited by Robert J. Alexander. Westport, Conn.: Greenwood Press, 1982, pp. 470–482.

––––––––. "Honduras: The Burden of Survival in Central America." In *Central America: Crisis and Adaptation,* edited by Steve C. Ropp and James A. Morris, Albuquerque: University of New Mexico Press, 1984, pp. 189–225.

Morris, James A., and Steve C. Ropp. "Corporatism and Dependent Development: A Honduran Case Study." *Latin American Research Review* 12, no. 2 (Summer 1977), pp. 27–68.

Morris, James A., and Marta Sánchez. "Factores de poder en la evolución politica del campesinado hondureño." *Estudios sociales centroamericanos* 6, no. 16 (January–April 1977), pp. 85–106.

Muller, Gene Alan. "The Church in Poverty: Bishops, Bourbons, and Tithes in Spanish Honduras, 1700–1821." Ph.D. dissertation, University of Kansas, 1981.

Murga Frassinetti, Antonio. *Enclave y sociedad en Honduras.* Tegucigalpa, D.C.: Universidad Nacional Autonoma de Honduras, 1978.

————. "Industrialización dependiente y capital imperialista en Honduras." *Cuadernos políticas* (Mexico), no. 31 (January–March 1983), pp. 58–71.

Nichols, John S. "Honduras." In *World Press Encyclopedia,* edited by George Thomas Kurian. New York: Facts on File, 1982, pp. 437–446.

Paredes, Lucas. *Drama político en Honduras.* México: Editora Latinoamericana, 1959.

————. *Liberalismo y nacionalismo (Transfugísmo político).* Tegucigalpa, D.C.: Imprenta Honduras, 1963.

Pearson, Neale J. "Peasant Pressure Groups and Agrarian Reform in Honduras, 1962–1977." In *Rural Change and Public Policy: Eastern Europe, Latin America, and Australia,* edited by William P. Avery et al. New York: Pergamon Press, 1980, pp. 297–320.

"Costa Rica, Honduras, and Panama." In *Communism in Central America and the Caribbean,* edited by Robert Wesson. Stanford: Hoover Institution Press, 1982, pp. 94–116.

————. "The 1980 and 1981 Honduran Elections; Manifestations of a Critical Realignment of Political Participation and Power." Paper presented at the Rocky Mountain Council on Latin American Studies meeting, Glendale, Ariz., March 1982.

Posas A., Mario. "Política estatal y estructura agraria en Honduras (1950–1978)." *Estudios sociales centroamericanos* 8, no. 24 (September–December 1979), pp. 37–116.

Posas A., Mario, and Rafael del Cid. "Honduras: Los limites del reformiso castrense (1972–1979)." *Revista mexicana de sociología* 42, no. 2 (April–June 1980), pp. 607–650.

————. *La construcción del sector público y del estado nacional de Honduras, 1876–1979.* San José: EDUCA, 1981.

Quiñónez, Edgardo, and Mario Argueta. *História de Honduras.* Tegucigalpa, D.C.: Escuela Superior del Profesorado "Francisco Morazán," 1978.

Reina, Jorge Arturo. "Honduras: ¿Revolución pacifica o violenta?" *Nueva Sociedad,* no. 54 (May–June 1981), pp. 35–56.

Ropp, Steve C. "The Honduran Army in the Sociopolitical Evolution of the Honduran State." *The Americas* 30, no. 4 (April 1974), pp. 504–528.

Rosenberg, Mark B. "Honduran Scorecard: Military and Democrats in Central America." *Caribbean Review* 12, no. 1 (Winter 1983), pp. 12–15, 40–42.

Rudolf, James D., ed. *Honduras, A Country Study.* Washington, D.C.: American University, 1984.

Ruhl, J. Mark. "Agrarian Structure and Political Stability in Honduras." *Journal of Inter-American Studies and World Affairs* 26, no. 1 (February 1984), pp. 33–68.

Salamon, Leticia. *Militarismo y reformiso en Honduras.* Tegucigalpa, D.C.: Editorial Guaymuras, 1982.

Santos M., Benjamín. *Díez años de lucha: Partido Demócrata Cristiano de Honduras.* Guatemala: Editorial INCEP, 1980.

Sierra Mejía, Marcio Enrique. "Dessarrollo capitalista y economías campesinas en la región occidental de Honduras." Thesis, Facultad de Ciencias Sociales, Universidad de Costa Rica, 1980.

Slutzky, Daniel, and Esther Alonso. *Empresas transnacionales y agricultura: El caso del enclave bananero en Honduras.* Tegucigalpa, D.C.: Editorial Universitaria, 1980.

Smith-Hinds, William Lorenzo. "Commitment and Community in a Honduran Campesino Organization." Ph.D. dissertation, University of Notre Dame, 1980.

Stokes, William S. *Honduras: An Area Study in Government.* Madison: University of Wisconsin Press, 1950.

————. "Honduras: Dilemma of Development." *Current History* 42, no. 246 (February 1962), pp. 83–88.

————. "Honduras: Problems and Prospects." *Current History* 50, no. 293 (January 1966), pp. 22–26.

Thompson, Joseph R. "An Economic Analysis of the Public Expenditure in Honduras, 1925–1963." Ph.D. dissertation, University of Florida, 1968.

Universidad Nacional Autonoma de Honduras. *Recopilación de las constituciones de Honduras, 1825–1965.* Tegucigalpa, D.C.: Editorial Universitaria, 1977.

Villanueva, Benjamín. "Institutional Innovation and Economic Development, Honduras: A Case Study." Ph.D. dissertation, University of Wisconsin, 1968.

White, Robert Anthony. *The Adult Education Program of Acción Cultural Hondureña: An Evaluation of the Rural Development Potential of the Radio School Movement in Honduras.* Full Report, pts. 1 and 2. St. Louis: St. Louis University, 1972.

————. "Structural Factors in Rural Development: The Church and Peasant in Honduras." Ph.D. dissertation, Cornell University, 1977.

West, Robert C., and John P. Augelli. *Middle America, Its Lands and Peoples.* 2d ed. Englewood Cliffs, N.J.: Prentice-Hall, 1976.

Woodward, Ralph Lee, Jr. *Central America: A Nation Divided.* New York: Oxford University Press, 1976.

————. "The Twilight of Liberalism in Central America: The Present Crisis in Historical Perspective." In *RMCLAS Proceedings*, edited by John J. Brasch and Susan R. Rouch. Rocky Mountain Council on Latin American Studies, 29th meeting, Las Cruces, 12–14 February 1981.

Zaldaña Lara, José, et. al. "El sistema político administrativo de la región centro-occidental (Comayagua)." Facultad de Ciencias Económicas, Universidad Nacional Autonoma de Honduras, 1980.

DOCUMENTS—REPUBLIC OF HONDURAS

Asamblea Nacional Constituyente. *Ley electoral y de las organizaciones políticas.* Decreto No. 53. Tegucigalpa, D.C.: República de Honduras, 20 April 1981.

————. "Constitución de la República." Decreto No. 131, 11 January 1982. *La Gaceta* 106, no. 23.612. Tegucigalpa, D.C.: 20 January 1982.

Banco Central de Honduras. *Honduras en cifras, 1978–1980.* Tegucigalpa, D.C.:
Departamento de Estudios Económicos, July 1981.
Diagnóstico de los recursos humanos, 1961–1974. Tegucigalpa, D.C.: Consejo Superior
de Planificación Económica, July 1976.
Dirección General de Estadística y Censos. *Censo nacional agropecuario, 1974.*
Tegucigalpa, D.C.: Ministerio de Economia, July 1979.
————. *Compendio estadístico, 1977.* Tegucigalpa, D.C.: Ministerio de Economia,
October 1979.
Dirección General de Estadística y Censos and Consejo Superior de Planificación
Económica. *Compendio estadístico, 1967/1968.* Tegucigalpa, D.C.: República
de Honduras, n.d.
Ley constitutiva de las Fuerzas Armadas de Honduras. Decreto No. 180, 30 January
1975. Tegucigalpa, D.C.: Departamento de Relaciones Públicas, 1975.
Instituto Nacional Agrario. *Resumen de datos generales del sector reformado.*
Tegucigalpa, D.C.: Departamento de Planificación, December 1978.
República de Honduras. *Ley de Reforma Agraria.* Decreto No. 170, 1 January
1975. Tegucigalpa, D.C.: República de Honduras, 1975.

DOCUMENTS—UNITED STATES

U.S. Agency for International Development (USAID). *Honduras: Country Devel-
opment Strategy Statement, FY 82.* Washington, D.C.: Government Printing
Office, January 1980.
————. *Country Development Strategy Statement, FY 83.* Washington, D.C.:
Government Printing Office, January 1981.
U.S. Congress, House, Subcommittee on Inter-American Affairs. "Salvadoran
Refugees in Honduras." *Hearing,* 97th Congress, 1st session, 17 December
1981.
U.S. Congress, House, Committee on Foreign Affairs. "Honduras and U.S.
Foreign Policy: An Emerging Dilemma." *Hearing,* 97th Congress, 2d session,
21 September 1982.
U.S. Congress, Senate, Committee on Foreign Relations. "The Honduran Sit-
uation." *Staff Report,* 97th Congress, 2d session, December 1982.

Index

151

About the Book and Author

HONDURAS
Caudillo Politics and Military Rulers
James A. Morris

Since the retirement of longtime dictator Tiburcio Carías Andino (1932–1949), the search for institutional stability in Honduras has led to both democratically elected governments and the imposed discipline of military rule. Social and economic change has contributed to the growth of middle-class urban groups, strongly organized labor unions, and a vigorous peasant movement. The Honduran armed forces, established in modern form only after World War II, filled the vacuum of political power that developed as the Liberal and National political parties failed to address the problems created by change and national development, but the authoritarianism of military rule has been countered by historical patterns of caudillo politics. Despite the revolutionary turmoil that surrounds the country, Hondurans have successfully conducted national elections and installed a freely elected civilian government after more than ten years of military rule. It is within this mix of "traditional" and "praetorian" governing modes that Hondurans have fashioned a style of politics conducive to compromise, which accounts for the country's relative tranquillity today.

In this first comprehensive study of contemporary Honduras—its land, people, economy, and politics—to be published in English, Dr. Morris also outlines the historical context that has shaped the society of this now geopolitically important nation and conditioned its political dynamics over the past three decades. His analysis illuminates the characteristics that distinguish Honduras from its Central American neighbors and that may dictate a unique course for its political evolution.

James A. Morris received his Ph.D. in 1974 from the University of New Mexico and has taught political science at several universities in the southwestern United States. He has written articles on Honduran politics for journals and periodicals; studied and traveled in Argentina, Uruguay, the Dominican Republic, Colombia, and Central America; and been a consultant to the Department of State. He is coeditor of *Central America: Crisis and Adaptation* (1984).